"Alexia has a keen understanding of the young professionals who are overwhelming the workforce. She is truly a master at developing their professional, communication, and leadership skills. Her intelligent coaching approach to understanding this segment of our workforce is timely and purposeful to the success of all sizes of companies. This wise, witty, and readable book should be required reading for everyone who is in HR or has management responsibility of young professionals. It is the definitive guide to onboarding and retaining young professionals in your company."

Jille Bartolome, MCC, president of Inner Beauty Institute

"Alexia is revolutionizing how we prepare new nurses for the demands of the workplace in Nevada. In *90 Days 90 Ways*, she shows she truly understands how to grow a new generation of ethical, high-impact communicators and leaders from day one. This will help employers increase efficiency while improving employee retention."

Doug Geinzer, CEO of So   alition

"Onboarding has been viewed for too long as an exercise in compliance versus an integral part of strategic planning. If you want to keep the talent you've worked so hard to attract, Alexia's words should extend well beyond HR to the highest levels of management."

Emily Bennington, author of *Effective Immediately: How to Fit In, Stand Out, and Move Up at Your First Real Job*

"Alexia Vernon has written a brilliant roadmap for onboarding success. *90 Days 90 Ways* is definitely a go-to book for those looking to make the most out of their current onboarding process as well as for those looking to create one that can help anchor the knowledge, skills, and abilities of new hires. Alexia's insight into both the needs of the employee and the needs of the organization are spot-on, and shows why Alexia is such a great thought leader in this area."

Jason Gardner, CPLP, Owner of FlipChart This and President of ASTD Greater Las Vegas

"Alexia offers up a fluid, fun, and insanely useful conversation for all hiring managers, HR professionals, and trainers. Studies show that the connectivity created in an employee's first 90 days is crucial, and this field guide for onboarding will help you ensure your practices set people up for success and satisfaction."

Lisa Haneberg, author of 12 business books, including *Coaching Up and Down the Generations*

90 Days 90 Ways

Onboard Young Professionals to Peak Performance

90 Days 90 Ways

Onboard Young Professionals
to Peak Performance

ALEXIA VERNON

ASTD
WORKPLACE LEARNING & PERFORMANCE
PRESS

ASTD Press is an internationally renowned source of insightful and practical information on workplace learning and performance topics, including training basics, evaluation and return on investment, instructional systems development, elearning, leadership, and career development. Visit us at www.astd.org/astdpress.

Ordering information: Books published by ASTD Press can be purchased by visiting our website at store.astd.org or by calling 800.628.2783 or 703.683.8100.

Library of Congress Control Number: 2012934023
ISBN-10: 1-56286-816-0
ISBN-13: 978-1-56286-816-1

ASTD Press Editorial Staff:
Director: Anthony Allen
Senior Manager, Production & Editorial: Glenn Saltzman
Project Manager, Content Acquisition: Kristin Husak
Associate Editor: Heidi Smith
Indexing: Abella Publishing Services, LLC
Cover Design: Ana Ilieva Foreman
Printed by: Victor Graphics, Inc., Baltimore, MD, www.victorgraphics.com

CONTENTS

Introduction

"Be daring, be different, be impractical, be anything that will assert integrity of purpose and imaginative vision against the play-it-safers, the creatures of the commonplace, the slaves of the ordinary."

Sir Cecil Beaton

If you have freely chosen to pick up this book—which I hope you have, for forced learning just like forced therapy rarely yields good results—you most likely employ, supervise, train, or are in some way responsible for the success of new hires. A large percentage of these employees are likely young professionals—by which I mean employees between the ages of 18–30. (The generation of employees born between 1978–2000, typically referred to as Generation Y or Millennials, will be the largest generation in the workplace by 2016.)

Unlike picking up this book, you may not have a lot of choice in who these young professionals are, and yet you are tasked with getting them "on board" and to peak performance by the end of their probationary period. Most likely there are a lot of forces working against you successfully completing this mission: other employees with competing interests and needs, a laundry list of your own responsibilities, or unfulfilled professional dreams that make you daydream and Internet search more than you would care to admit. And then there's the term "onboarding" itself. It's yet another piece of jargon you're supposed to care about.

So you've half-heartedly picked up tips wherever you could find them on this onboarding thing—which I'm defining as "getting new employees oriented, integrated, and delivering results as efficiently, effectively, and energetically as possible." Chances are we've read some of the same books and articles that touch upon how to do this.

"Help new employees understand who you are as a company so they are prepared on the day they start to integrate into the company."

Carmen Marston,
VP of Human Resources at Zimmerman Advertising, as featured in *Workforce* magazine

"Make sure that all stakeholders are involved in the onboarding process. This should include hiring, training, HR, and any internal coaches."

Talya Bauer's 2010 "Onboarding New Employees: Maximizing Success"
SHRM report

"This generation is showing up totally aware of work-life balance. They value time with family and friends, and they value their time doing things they enjoy. Boomers and Gen X employees typically didn't ask for 'balance' until they had been in the workforce for 15+ years. Millennials are requesting it from day one. And, the smart companies are offering it."

Lisa Orrell,
Author of the book *Millennials Incorporated*, as featured on JobDig.com

"Be authentic with your Gen Y employees."

G.L. Hoffman's *U.S. News and World Report* article,
"How to Get Rock-Star Employees On Board in the New Normal"

Perhaps you even agree with a lot of what you have read. Yet if you are anything like me you feel that while it may be relatively easy to get on board with some of the concepts, implementing them is a whole different beast. And if we are similar, you probably also don't just want to "follow the rules." Sure, you are interested in employing best practices. Yet there is so much discussion in management and in learning and development about creating cultures of risk-taking, innovation, and outright play. Even if you haven't completely bought in, you're eager to—dare I say it—incorporate some Full Unadulterated Nonsense (FUN) from time-to-time into your onboarding.

If what I'm saying is resonating, then keep reading. (And if it's not, well, return the book if the spine is still intact, give it to a more adventurous colleague, or if all else fails, use it as a coaster on your desk or coffee table.) I've written this book for the folks who have the desire to more efficiently, effectively, and enthusiastically onboard their youngest employees, with a toolbox full of strategies and techniques that make the murky vision a crystal clear reality. As a speaker, trainer, and ICF certified coach who specializes in empowering young professionals (and those who recruit, manage, train, and lead them) to sustainable workplace success, I've spent the last decade helping people identify and employ the necessary action-oriented strategies to transfer into action the kind of quick and dirty tips that get trafficked in the media, sometimes by people like me.

Also, I'm a Millennial. (I don't confess this to many people, but I'm already dying my gray roots, so please rest assured I am on the older side of the generation!) I share this to model the young professional value of transparency. I also want you to know that in addition to my professional experience addressing action-oriented solutions with corporations, small businesses, nonprofit organizations, universities, and professional associations in a wide-range of industries such as education, workforce development, healthcare, social enterprise, and real estate, I have generational credibility or "gen-cred". To support you in Sir Beaton's charge to be "daring, different, and impractical" while obtaining the results you seek, throughout the book I will help you get inside the minds of your youngest employees. For when you are able to meet your young new hires where they are, then you will be able to co-create a mutually agreed upon pathway for success.

Before we dive in, though, there are a few ground rules to ensure that we play together nicely. First, I'm going to ask you to let go of any complaining you have done in thought or deed regarding your young professionals. Todd Hudson, the founder of the Maverick Institute, compares training the Millennial generation to moving through Elizabeth Kubler-Ross's five stages of grief. By opening this book, chances are you've at least moved through the first stage, denial. You understand that this onboarding thing matters. You may be hanging out in stage two, though, anger. You believe it's a bunch of malarkey that you have to adapt the way you bring on new employees for the newest generation of employees. "These little beasts should be kissing my feet every day because they have a job," you think to yourself. Or perhaps you're even in the third stage, bargaining. You'd do anything to make this onboarding thing someone else's responsibility. You're tired. You're overworked. You're a lot of things—now suddenly an onboarder. Finally, perhaps you've moved through these earlier stages and now you're at stage four, depression. You need a big infusion of energy and enthusiasm to do this latest work you are tasked with.

My goal, wherever you are, is to get you to stage five, acceptance, as quickly as possible. *But I've had so many employees who have caused problems. Aren't I entitled to a light drizzle of complaint?* No. While in a perfect world recruiters and hiring managers would be able to select "good fits," as we know, this is often not the case. And if you think back to your early employment days, I suspect it's fair to say that you look a lot different today than you did back then. If you want to take a young professional from new hire to knockout employee—which as I'll prove to you again and again is in your best interest—you've got to be prepared in mind, skills, and spirit to do the work from the moment that new employee walks in the door. An obstacle-centered perspective gets you in your own way of recognizing opportunities for improvement and creates an us-versus-them mentality that perpetuates workplace intergenerational conflict. And workplace intergenerational conflict is rampant! In a recent poll conducted by the Society for Human Resource Management (SHRM), 44 percent of managers of young employees reported that it exists to some degree in their organizations.

Second, for us to build castles in the sand, I need you to be open to trying new ways, not only of thinking but also of acting. Change usually feels a little strange until we make our behavior into a new habit. While you do not have to add each tactic I share to your onboarding toolbox, I'm going to ask you to approach each one with an open mind, try it out a few times, and then and only then—if it's just not working for you or your young professionals—put it away.

Finally—and you can blame this on both the trainer and the Millennial in me—I think the best learning is dialogical. This book is not just mine to write; it's also yours. So as you read, please allow my recommendations, experiences, examples, and other musings to jumpstart a chain reaction of ideas and actions from you. Write any and all "ahas" in the margins. Share excerpts and specific tactics or examples with your staff, colleagues, and other thought leaders—referencing me if you would be so kind. Dare to deviate from my prescriptions in service of coming up with your own best medicine.

We will start our adventure together by exploring what you need to know about the newest crop of young professionals for you and your company to forge a mutually beneficial relationship with them. I will differentiate between the post-grad (whether grad is high school or college for your young professional population) habits you want to keep and the habits you want to break, look at this generation's coming of age experiences and attitudes, and demystify how they think about and like to perform their work. Then, in the following nine chapters, I will show you how to:

- Design an effective first-day experience for your new young professional.

- Identify and communicate the most important information needed to be successful, such as chief position responsibilities and accountabilities, organizational short- and long-term goals, and the chain of command.

- Integrate your new hires into your workplace culture.

- Develop a new generation of employees who consistently communicate for maximum impact.

- Create employees who deliver results, learn and grow from mistakes, and are accountable.

- Keep young professionals focused on their priorities and efficient in their work.

- Model and teach relationship building and service-orientation within and outside your four walls.

- Weed out new hire stress and anxiety through such tactics as helping employees create a possibility-centered mindset, encouraging autonomy, and fostering work-life integration.

- Empower peak performance and grow the next generation of leaders.

In addition to introducing you to 10 tactics that will allow you and your onboarding team to implement each best practice within a new hire's first 90 days, you will also hear from young professionals at companies with great formal and informal onboarding practices. I have also sprinkled throughout tips from managers, trainers, human resources professionals, and consultants who "get" how to efficiently and effectively onboard young professionals. So that you can easily spot key information, the following logos will appear from chapter 2 on.

Which Day(s) to Prioritize Tactic

This is an actionable way to carry out the guiding principle in each chapter. Although it would have been equal parts clever and tidy for the chapters and tactics to have been presented in chronological order, as you know if you are engaged in this work, much of it overlaps and should continue once started. To support you in implementing the information, I've given some general parameters around when to begin employing each tactic.

Distinction

To ensure that we are on the same page, I often differentiate between complementary yet distinct concepts. My hope is that by understanding the nuances between ideas and practices, you can best incorporate the tactics into your young professional onboarding arsenal.

Definition

A lot of jargon gets bandied around in the business world. I'm as guilty of it as anyone else. To ensure you know what I mean when I'm introducing what I deem an important word or phrase, I share what each means to me.

Role Play

My background in theatre and drama has always been a cornerstone of my training and coaching. Even when we are not up and rehearsing on our feet, I believe that by understanding a scenario and the characters involved in a role play, we empower ourselves to translate a practice into effective action. So I use sample role plays when I think a tactic could benefit from being fleshed out.

Tweet-Sized Takeaway

For those of you who suffer from or have freely adopted social media apathy, Twitter is an online social networking and microblogging site that allows users to communicate in real time by reading and sending messages that are up to140 characters. According to *The Atlantic*, by the end of 2010, 29 percent of Twitter users were ages 18–25, and the second largest demographic, coming in at 23 percent, were ages 26–34. Whether your young professionals use Twitter or not, as we will explore, young professionals like and respond to easy-to-digest sound bites. To groom you, I'm closing each chapter with takeaways that are 140 characters or less! (**And if you are on Twitter or are simply ready to dive into the social medium, you can follow me @ AlexiaVernon and use the hashtag #90d90w to let me know what you think of the book**.) Also, if there's a tweet-sized takeaway that is really working for you, you can tweet it yourself!

Although I'm talking about members of my generation, you will also notice that throughout the book I refer to young professionals in the third person rather than in the first person plural. I do this because while I think my age gives you a window into your young employee's thoughts, feelings, behaviors, habits, and so forth, I'm writing this book for you. Positioning myself as one of them would distance me from you and get confusing.

Finally, let's revisit that notion of FUN. I believe wholeheartedly that learning and results are predicated on the people involved having the payoff for their achievement at the top of their minds. And although we often think of payoff as being somewhat future-oriented, I believe that the best rewards happen in real time when we're enjoying ourselves. While I think the subject of onboarding young professionals—who, as the next generation of our leaders will be charged with some gigantic tasks in the years ahead—is important business, I also know that you will be more likely to transfer what I'm saying into action if you enjoy reading it and have opportunities to laugh throughout. So you will notice that I'll be pretty playful during our time together!

Now, you have agreed to the ground rules. You know where we are going. You are clear on why I'm writing as I do. So let's head on over to chapter 1 and demystify your newest generation of employees so that you understand how to best onboard them for sustainable success.

chapter 1:
Young Professional 411

"Give me ownership in my work
and involvement and I'll give my all."

GenBlending.com

"They are the soul of my company—always providing fresh ideas and fixes for problems that the rest of us are too set in our ways to see."

"I couldn't believe how unbelievably rude he was. After showing up over 30 minutes late to a mandatory all-day training, he proceeds to be on his phone all morning. When I told him that if he was unwilling or unable to participate he could leave, he did! And then I got a call the next day from his mom chewing me out for my behavior."

"They are constant learners. Always wanting more training, more mentoring, and more opportunities to grow in their role."

Each of these unnamed managers or trainers is describing a young professional. While it may border on unfathomable that members of the same generation can be branded creative, collaborative, and tech savvy, along with disrespectful, entitled, and downright whiny, they consistently are—and it's for a good reason. Our newest crop of young professionals have almost as many things that differentiate them as they have things in common. For example, this generation is simultaneously referred to as incredibly educated and yet ill prepared for the workplace. And here again, the media is essentially spot on. While 60 percent of this generation enrolls in college—and it's worth noting that this is the first generation where women are outnumbering men in degrees earned—it's important to dig deeper to see the disparity in this generation's educational outcomes. For example, 70 percent of young white Americans (approximately 56 percent of the population in America) graduate high school in four years. When demographers report that young professionals are earning more advanced degrees and are postponing full-time professional employment longer than any previous generation, they are referring to young professionals who have the privilege to stay in school, travel the world, pursue a series of non-paying internships, and live with ma and pa as long as needed. These are usually white, middle- to upper-class Americans.

Approximately 40 percent of young professionals are minorities, and the coming-of-age stereotypes of scheduled playdates and near constant parental intervention often don't apply to them. For example, only 55 percent of African American students (approximately 15 percent of this generation) graduate high school in four years. Of those who matriculate, just over 40 percent graduate from college; most enter the workplace right after high school or concurrent to pursuing a college degree. Their parents usually do not accompany them to job interviews or call their supervisors for performance updates.

Although young professionals are diverse in educational background and privilege, there are still key similarities to be aware of and to use in your onboarding strategy. Of the thousands of young professionals I have trained, spoken with, and befriended–for remember, I am of the same age as the generation of which I speak—I have found a number of key motivators. While I cover these in more depth in chapter 6, one motivator is paramount and needs to be considered before a young professional ever walks in your door: engagement. When young professionals feel ownership over their work and understand how it affects others—fellow staff, clients and customers, and the community at large—they stay engaged. Period. In the words of Tyler Durbin, the lead author and editor of the popular site, GenYJourney.com, "Don't just hire a young person because there is an open position. Hire them at a time when management can make an investment in them. There is nothing worse for onboarding a new hire than bringing them on board and then not giving them the time and resources they need to succeed."

Your number one imperative as someone responsible for young professionals' success during the onboarding process is to get them clear on their work and its contribution to other people as quickly and cleverly as possible.

Beyond their similarities in motivation, young professionals will typically show up to your company with many if not all of the following "things" in common (values, habits, desires, and beliefs) shaped not only by upbringing, which can be hard to generalize, but also by what they have experienced based on the period in history in which they have come of age.

Young professionals think about work in a fundamentally different way than previous generations. While the Bureau of Labor Statistics (BLS) says that Baby Boomers—the largest generation in the workplace for at least another few years—will hold an average of 10–11 jobs throughout their careers, the BLS predicts our newest young professionals will have approximately nine jobs just by the age of 32. And according to a recent Lumin Collaborative survey, nowhere do these statistics play out more clearly than within your four walls. Most likely, 40 percent of your young professionals have been in their jobs less than a year (compared to only 8 percent of employees from other generations).

To be sure, there are some young professionals who lust for steady employment with one company, a robust 401k, and ample vacation time. These are the young professionals rushing into the county, city, state, and federal government jobs that are left. The vast majority of young professionals, however, recognize that working for one or even just a few employers is unrealistic in the 21st century workplace. According to the Pew Research Center, between 35–40 percent of young professionals lost employment during the recession.

Young professionals are therefore adopting an entrepreneurial approach to their career development; they always have an eye toward where the opportunities lie, and how they can marry their values, strengths, interests, and experiences with them as well as build the relationships they need to make sustainable employment on their terms happen. If and when such opportunities do not emerge with an established company, or they identify a market need that has yet to have been met (or one they feel they can meet better), young professionals have no problem starting up their own business or piecing together a variety of consulting gigs or multiple streams of income.

Ironically, despite their discovery that they can be the first employees to be let go from their companies, most young professionals are incredibly loyal to employers whom they respect, for whom they feel they can make an impact, and who give them work that engages them. It is not uncommon to find such young professionals showing up before and staying long after their managers and senior leaders to ensure that a project they care about happens. In fact, the number one reason a young professional willingly leaves her job is because she feels like she can no longer learn or grow in her role.

I do not advise you to measure the success of your young professional onboarding on retention alone, as it is no longer practical for a young professional to invest her career or even a number of years with just one company. However, as we'll explore in the coming chapters, understanding young professionals' motivators, goals, and strengths will enable you to maximize their contribution while they do reside within your four walls, to minimize intergenerational conflict and decreased productivity, and to create an environment with an eye toward innovation and sustainable growth.

Young professionals use communication and technology for efficiency...and often at the expense of accuracy. Unless you have been living solo in a cave without Internet or cell phone access for the last decade, you are already well aware that our newest generation of workplace professionals likes technology (even if their use of it is not as sophisticated as it is for the generation just before them, Generation X). Fafie Moore, the owner of Realty Executives Nevada, refers to the newest generation in the workplace as "screen babies." Just minutes after sliding out of their mothers' wombs, they were placed in front of a TV for their infotainment. (In kindergarten I remember typing in my class on an Apple IIe. Yes, I was typing letters before I even knew how to read!)

And again, assuming you haven't been trapped in that cave, you've seen more than your fair share of 18–32 year olds texting on their cell phones to ask someone out, break up with them, propose to them, and break up with them again, as well as to let their supervisors know they will be running late. After all, many young professionals don't wear watches. They use smartphones to keep time. And because when young professionals are engaged they are really engaged, one might even text during the weekend or in the middle of the night to ask you a burning question about a project or share an idea that came from a dream. Yet, because of young professionals' overreliance on cute and not so tidy abbreviations, for example: AWSUM ID-A. 4 R. K. TTFN, you may have absolutely no idea what she is trying to say. ("Awesome idea. For Thursday. Okay. Ta-ta for now" if you were lost!)

If you currently work with a lot of young professionals, you know that if you want a fast response, you text the question or send it as a Facebook message. You never leave a voicemail. Most young professionals just don't retrieve them. And in the wake of Facebook status updates and Twitter, even when you communicate with your young professionals over the phone or—dare I suggest it—face-to-face, you need to spit out your information in 10 seconds or less. Otherwise your young professional has moved on without you coming along for the ride.

Because of this reliance on technology and the shift away from old-fashioned oral communication that has come with it, I'm sure you know that your young professionals cannot compete with their predecessors in their face-to-face communication skills. Their spoken and written grammar is equally atrocious. And yet in our increasingly service-oriented society, it's quite likely that the key customer service functions in your company are performed by people you least want to have as a mirror for your company's ability to communicate. Young professionals answer inquiry calls, open doors, deliver goods, and handle complaints and returns.

If this is resonating for you and you feel sweat starting to drip from your brow or a panic attack coming on, take a deep breath. I assure you we're going to explore how you can effectively onboard your young professionals to be both tech and communication rock stars within their first 90 days. We just have to put our attention on the skills that need development, and take the time to make it a priority and a reality.

Young professionals care as much about lifestyle as paycheck. Coming of age at the height of the self-help movement, our newest young professionals recite Oprah and Dr. Phil quotes as part of their everyday speech. *Breathe and let go. Follow your instincts. Anger is nothing more than an outward expression of hurt, fear, and frustration.* Irrespective of whether they find themselves flipping burgers or filing expense reports, they have also internalized the message that work should be inherently meaningful. Happiness should be a universal workplace right. As someone who works and loves life at the intersections of coaching, training, leadership, and positive psychology, I think my generation has gotten this belief right. We know that American companies lose about $300 billion each year due to workplace stress—which I'm defining as damaging physical, social, and emotional reactions that occur when one lacks the abilities and resources to complete her job requirements. Employees who are stressed cost us money from their mistakes, absences, health problems, and turnover. On the flip side, companies with the happiest and engaged employees make our companies big bucks. The top 10 in 2010 according to Forbes.com are: Adobe, American Express, Google, IBM, KPMG, PepsiCo, Southwest Airlines, Starbucks, UBS, and Zappos.

According to Jobtrak.com, 42 percent of recent graduates report that a meaningful life outside of work is the most important criteria in determining how to develop their careers. Valuing lifestyle over payment, young professionals often move to cities and choose organizations and roles where they can play as hard as they work. Most young professionals have let go of the unattainable goal of work-life balance. While math may not be a generational strength, most young professionals understand that if you work 8–10 hours/day over 5–6 days/week, sleep another 6–8 hours/day, that remaining life piece just isn't going to be equal to the work one. So young professionals look for and stay in work situations where they can have time for—and perhaps some compensation toward—exercise; where they can have a sense of play infused in their actual workday; and where they can have a few floating holidays to volunteer for a social cause they are passionate about. As you will learn, when your onboarding practices create a culture of happiness and engagement that employees continue to enjoy after their orientation period, it's a win-win for the entire company.

WHY THE FOCUS ON 90 DAYS

Ninety is a magical number. It's the amount of days most new hires have to lay the foundation for success in their companies. It's the span of time five major war battles—Barents Sea, Guadalcanal, El Alamein, Operation Torch, and Stalingrad—changed the course of history by bringing an end to World War II. Just as importantly, according to positive psychologists, it's also the approximate amount of days it takes to make a new habit a way of being. Whether somebody is weeding out carbs from her diet, developing patience, or eradicating "like" from her everyday speech, neuroscience proves it takes about 90 days to make it happen. Now that you know what drives a lot of your young professional new hires, I want to share with you some quick and dirty tips about the key habits you want them to keep and the key habits you want to reshape during your onboarding process.

HABITS TO KEEP

Balancing Multiple "Things"

While multitasking is rarely an effective use of an employee's time, knowing how to move back and forth intentionally from one activity to another is. Due to their very programmed childhoods and college years—after school sports, drama club, student council, community service, test prep—and the shift in entertainment and media away from linear narratives to quick sketches and multiple plotlines, many young professionals are quite skilled at shifting their focus to a new focus within a matter of minutes. While they often have sacrificed significant paid work experience to pursue myriad extracurricular pursuits, their ability to shift gears at a moment's notice and commit to multiple "things"—be they projects or ideas—is one to capitalize on.

Collaboration

Beginning from when they were making mud pies on the playground and continuing up to when they were presenting their college capstone projects, young professionals have been working in teams. You want to continue this approach to work because it is comfortable for most young professionals. By feeling a sense of community at work, your young professionals will feel more engaged in what they do and have people to turn to for guidance and support as they work out the inevitable kinks in performing their new roles.

Respect for Difference

Your young professionals have grown up in the most diverse generation in history. This goes deeper than a mere appreciation for different sexes, genders, races, cultures, religions, sexual orientations, geographies, abilities, and so forth. Bombarded by the message that being different gets you recognized—and consistently lauded for trailblazing—young professionals enjoy working with people who exhibit different ways of thinking, creating, communicating, leading, and problem solving. Tap this desire for genuine diversity both by allowing your young professionals to hold on to their authentic selves (even if you have a hard time seeing them underneath the tattoos and piercings) and by letting them rub off on existing employees who may foreclose the healthy need for multiple ways of seeing, believing, and behaving.

Commitment to Learning

By the time many young professionals enter the workplace, many have been in school for 19 years. And that's if they graduated college in just four years and don't have an advanced degree. Your young professionals have most definitely made a habit of learning, and you have a real opportunity to frame the work they are engaged in as a continuation of their previous education. Helping your youngest new hires see opportunities to grow once they understand their roles—for unlike school, they may not have a lot of new material to continue to master once they have been fully oriented—will help them stay motivated, focused, and on track for potential promotion.

Recycle-the-Box™ Thinking

Although Recycle-the-Box™ is a term I coined, nobody does it more naturally than the newest generation of young professionals. By which I mean, young professionals don't just think "outside the box." They throw the darn box up in the air and don't hold on to it until they are able to remake it into a solution that solves a problem—which sometimes you didn't even know existed—in a way that usually not only makes but also saves money. It typically makes people happy and is for the greater good. It's no accident that this is the generation that birthed Facebook, Zappos, and Gmail. Young professionals seem to have innovation wired into their DNA. While I'm not saying young professionals should be put into roles where they are charged to innovate all day long, you do want to give them freedom to rethink how their own work is completed and encourage the appropriate expression of ideas for both department and company improvement. Oftentimes their new vantage point can shine a light on blind spots more senior employees can no longer see.

HABITS TO RESHAPE

All-Nighters

Beginning in high school and typically continuing through college—irrespective of generation—young people have a tendency to deprioritize sleep. Because of a combination of procrastination, studying, overcommitting to people and projects, and usually a fair amount of partying, young people throw back some coffee, pop in some red-eye reduction drops, and live many of their weekdays on just a few hours of sleep. This might work when you only need to be "on" for a few hours of class each day. Exhaustion on a 9–5 schedule, however, just isn't sustainable. Encourage the development of healthy workplace habits with respect to time, energy maintenance, and stress management so that your young professionals can transfer them over into their personal lives.

Senioritis

The all-nighter can often be a symptom of a larger condition known as senioritis. Although most young professionals don't "graduate" on to anything at the end of their first 90 days or at the start of summer, the lack of motivation and concentration, as well as decreased performance and engagement, coupled with excessive tardiness and absence (key features of senioritis) can crop up around holidays and at the end of May. This is the time when young professionals recently out of school are used to the end of a marking period and the start of a vacation. Being aware of when these lulls are likely to happen and identifying the signs, if and when they emerge, enables you to have honest conversations with your young professionals about what is going on with them. It also gives you opportunities to co-create strategies for re-energizing them in their work.

The "What's My Grade?" Mentality

One of the drawbacks of those 19 or so years of schooling is that your young professionals are used to receiving a grade on their performance every quarter or semester. Oftentimes this translates into mediocre and at times subpar performance once the requirements for a satisfactory grade have been achieved. You want to curb this habit immediately. Not only do you not want to be in the business of assigning a grade to professional work—and as we will discuss in detail in chapter 6, giving ongoing feedback is the effective way to solidify what you want and quickly reshape what you don't—you also don't want employees whose sole motivation is to get work "done." We will look at performance metrics that shift quantitative assessment, like excellent, good, fair, and poor or A, B, C, D, F, to measurements that account for results, impact, and learning.

Success Is About the Individual

Even though young professionals have worked in teams, another drawback of their many years of education is that they are used to being assessed ultimately on their own performance. This has bred professionals who often show up to workplaces feeling like they have to compete to get noticed. If this attitude is left unchecked, it can spiral into employees who get in their own and others' way of success by not focusing their eye on how to make a team or department look good.

The Loudest One Wins

Young professionals who continue to see success as an individual achievement and who are therefore hungry for face time may also come across as ill-informed, inappropriate, or downright abrasive in their communication. Remember, this is the generation that was graded on their level of performance in classroom discussions. Oftentimes quantity and not quality were the indicators of this grade. I saw this all too often when I taught at the university level for a number of years—students simply regurgitating exactly what an author or classmate said or expressing their opinion without forwarding or deepening a conversation. We will look, particularly in chapter 5, at how to show your young professionals to speak with—rather than at—people as well as when and how it is appropriate to provide feedback.

Is your head whirling like a dervish yet? Please don't worry if you are still musing on exactly how you will either foster or reframe these habits. My intention was to open the window into seeing your young professionals anew. And now in the chapters that come, I'll be serving up nine guiding principles and 90 practical ways for you to consistently engage in onboarding them successfully. As I hope you are seeing, onboarding is not something that happens in a new hire orientation or a one-day class. It's a holistic and ongoing process that necessitates buy-in and work from anyone who has a stake in your new young professional's success. It's a marathon and not a sprint. It requires a lot of small, overlapping, and intentional steps in the way that you think and behave. It begins from the moment your new hire accepts her position.

And just in case you are asking yourself if you should even bother adapting or, if this is new to you, if you are considering how you will onboard your newest generation of employees, chew on this. While you might think that as 50 percent of the workplace population by 2014 (according to Tony Bingham), you can have your pick of young professionals, keep in mind a sobering statistic. According to Mark A. Stein and Lilith Christiansen, authors of the book *Successful Onboarding*, the average company experiences 13 percent attrition of its new hires within the first year.

While employing the tactics in this book will not weed out all attrition, for it is good and healthy to lose employees who are not the right fit, it will enable you to hold on to the right ones to save money and get back to your charge of driving business results. According to the Wynhurst Group, a boutique HR consultancy firm, 22 percent of staff turnover occurs in the first 45 days of employment, but new employees who go through a structured onboarding program are 58 percent more likely to be with an organization after three years. And the cost of losing an employee in the first year is at least three times her salary. As young professional onboarding expert Emily Bennington points out: "It makes no sense for businesses to spend an extraordinary amount of time and resources trying to recruit the best candidates, and then leave them alone to 'sink-or-swim' once they're hired. High turnover ripples out to all aspects of the business. For example, if your executives are constantly focused on hiring new staff, that's focus shifted away from taking care of clients." That's focus shifted away from leading! So, how have I done convincing you to turn the page and dive into chapter 2? Are you ready to explore how to design a first day experience for your new hires that lays the foundation for the rest of your onboarding efforts?

chapter 2:

Create a Knockout Day One

"Gen Y decides to stay—or not—
on our first day at work."

Jason Ryan Dorsey

A TALE OF TWO FIRST DAYS

Sam

"Good morning," Sam says to a young professional new hire. "I'm thrilled
to have you on the team." As the new employee looks to put down a bag,
Sam warns, "Don't get too comfortable just yet. You've got to check in with
HR first." Sam drops the employee off down the hall and over the next three

hours, the new employee is taken page by page through the new hire manual, learning a range of information from appropriate hand washing protocol to procedures for being vested after three years. Then, the employee returns to Sam's office to find a note sitting on top of a $10 bill that reads, "I'll be out at a meeting until after lunch. There's a great pizza place downstairs. It's on me." On the way back up the elevator after grabbing a bite, the employee overhears a conversation between two other young people. "I hear Sam's being courted by [*insert name of a competitor*]." "Yeah, doesn't surprise me. Sam's had one foot out the door for the last three years. Who doesn't?" When the elevator opens, the new employee watches as the two people talking exit and make their way into an office just a few doors down. Until Sam returns, the new employee goes back to Sam's office and begins flipping through the new hire manual, although by this point the new hire is really just turning the pages to appear busy to the other people who occasionally walk in and out of the office. People say "Hi," but nobody makes an introduction. Finally, Sam returns and says, "Let's get your computer all set up." Sam calls IT and then explains, "I've got another meeting at 2 p.m. that I'll be in the rest of the day. I'm so sorry that we haven't had a chance to chat. Feel free to leave once you have the technology orientation and then we'll have a proper first day tomorrow. I hope. My schedule has just been a little insane around here."

Chris

"Good morning," Chris says to a young professional new hire. "Nice to see you again." (*Note: Chris already brought the employee in for a one-on-one lunch the week before to have a relaxed, introductory conversation and get a lay of the land. During this time, Chris introduced the new hire to the other people in the department, the three senior level managers the employee would work with, and HR. Chris also gave a tour of the office and had the employee go home to watch the company's new hire video, accessible online with an employee username and password. The new employee also already participated at home in a webinar to get acquainted with position responsibilities and accountabilities.)* The young professional feels comfortable with Chris and says, "I'm really excited to be here. I had a chance to go through everything, and I've got just a few questions, a lot of ideas—when you are ready to hear them—and I can't wait to dive in." "Great," Chris says. "Let's sit down, go over your questions, and then I'll share with you the focus of the week. Also, I remember that you mentioned you like graphic design. I have a meeting later today and need to do something with my PowerPoint. Would you mind taking a look at it, and help me spruce up the template?" "That would be great," the new employee responds. The two take a little over an hour to address the new employee's questions and go over the top objective for the week, identifying three prospective referral partners, and then Chris has the new employee work on the PowerPoint template. Chris suggests that the new employee break for lunch at the same time as two other recent hires and plans a team lunch for the department the next day. In the afternoon, Chris and the new employee share their expectations for one another, their preferred learning and communication styles, and identify some criteria for giving and receiving feedback. Chris brings the new hire to the afternoon meeting with the task of writing down the top three takeaways. At the meeting, Chris acknowledges the employee for co-designing the PowerPoint presentation. Afterward Chris asks the employee to share the meeting takeaways and then to summarize the top two things about the role that are generating excitement and the top two things that are producing anxiety or dread. Chris explains that this information will guide the distribution of team tasks over the next 90 days. Finally, the new hire goes home for the day.

The preceding scenarios reflect two distinct approaches to onboarding a new young professional employee. In the first, Sam, while friendly and well-intentioned, has given little consideration to how a new employee will move through the day and patch together an impression of the company's culture and her role in it. Chris, on the other hand, has ensured that the first day experience gives a new employee an opportunity to take a deep dive into the new position, build relationships, and immediately have an opportunity to do the work she does best. I hope it doesn't surprise you that young professionals much prefer a Chris over a Sam. However, I hope it does shake you up to learn that these initial impressions will shape how new employees show up to work each day moving forward. You should also be aware that Sam is likely to lose the new recruit in less than a year; the new recruit has most likely decided by the end of day one to start planting seeds for how to get out the door and on to what's next. Chris, on the other hand, is likely to hold on to the new employee for...well, years. Chris's young employees are likely still working in Chris's company, and are probably taking on new positions with increased responsibility. When a young professional creates a first impression (that is solidified in the days and weeks to come) that she is an employee who will be valued, have opportunities to be engaged in her role and make an impact, can continually learn and grow, and is able to freely share her opinion with colleagues, she is likely to be one of the most loyal employees you will ever find.

At one of the few companies I worked for before launching my own business, I had two consecutive supervisors just like Sam. They were some of the nicest and smartest people in the world, just not so hot at onboarding. In my first role, I learned in less than a week that my supervisor was on the move, as were about a quarter of the staff once the company moved across town. I had my first day much to myself—with the exception of several long hours cooped up with my HR Director in the back of an office in a stuffy room that "closet" would be too kind of a descriptor for—filling out more paperwork than would have been required to join the CIA. I never took a lunch break because nobody offered me one. Once promoted, the experience pretty much repeated itself; another long trip to what I now knew everyone called "the cave." And this go-round I learned on my first day that my direct manager had already hatched an exit plan and was willing to have me take on as many of her responsibilities as I wanted.

These experiences turned out to be a stellar thing for me. They enabled me to climb an internal ladder that eluded many of my peers—all the while recording my musings on what was not working for us recent grads and devising my own plan for how I would make an impact in other organizations once I harnessed the chutzpah and money to hang up my own shingle. For most young professionals, though, a less than stellar first day does not have such a happy ending. Young professionals let the sour taste in their mouth spread like chicken pox. First, it creates an insatiable itch…to leave. And unless that young professional finds a balm quickly—by which I mean a new job—her itchiness spreads to her peers. Pretty soon you've got a tribe of dissatisfied young employees engaging in a constant drizzle of complaining, underperforming, and getting in the way of your company achieving—let alone growing—to the next level of success.

Creating a knockout first day experience for a young professional isn't brain surgery. However, it does require using a scalpel to know exactly what gunk you need to scrape off of what has become the typical first day experience. What remains should hook your young professionals and keep them coming back, delivering results, and driving your company forward. Now, without further ado, it's time to start filling your onboarding toolbox with the tactics to do all of this.

BEGIN DAY ONE PRIOR TO DAY ONE

In order for a young professional to have the opportunity to experience the recommendations proposed in the forthcoming tactics, as we saw in the example with Chris, a young professional needs to get a lot of the requisite new job info prior to coming in to work on the first day. I recommend—as does the Human Capital Institute and a host of other talent development organizations—making as much of it virtual as possible. Your young professionals are familiar and comfortable with accessing information they care about via blogs, videos, and webinars on their laptops and smartphones.

By putting your HR info, company history, role description, and so forth into these platforms, you send a lot of positive messages to your young professionals. You respect their time. You understand how they access content. You care about environmental sustainability. And you give your company hip points. You save "the first day" for connecting with your employee and clarifying anything that is confusing or anxiety-producing rather than for dumping information on her. If possible, get your young professional's work email address and login information set up in advance. There's nothing more frustrating for young professionals staring at a computer—as constant of a presence in their lives as water, food, sunlight, parents, and reality TV—and not being able to use it.

Ideally you have also had some kind of face-to-face contact with your young professionals before day one if you are their direct supervisor. And taking a cue from Chris, I hope you have also brought them in to give them a look at the lay of the land, introduce them to the other people they will be working closely with, and have given them an overview of their first day so they know what to expect. While you may not need to include what to wear and what not to wear with your more seasoned professionals (including shoes, accessories, piercings and tattoos); the time to arrive (and stay until); what to call senior leadership (Ms. Chang and not Christine); and what is (and isn't) appropriate for decorating a workspace, you do want to share this information with your young professional to set both of you up for success. If you can do it in a clever video performed by other young professionals in your workplace, all the better! And finally, make sure you know how to pronounce and spell your employee's name. Nothing sends a greater signal to young professionals that they are not valued than to have people, particularly a supervisor, not know who they are.

Chad Thompson, PhD, and Pat Caputo, PhD, both senior consultants at Aon Consulting, Inc., frame onboarding as a transition or break point—a time when one moves from the familiar to the unfamiliar or from a place of knowing to a place of questioning. For young professionals—who yes, are the first generation to have attended college in their jammies and had their parents call teachers to intervene on their behalf when they experienced bullying, or gossip, or sometimes a teacher who mispronounced their name or shot them a glance they didn't like—the first quarter of their life has been designed specifically to mitigate against discomfort. I don't think discomfort is a bad thing. Actually, it's where the majority of us do our greatest learning and growth. But it takes baby steps in order for those with risk aversion to swim rather than sink. The first day in a first or second full-time job is not when you want a young professional to feel alone at sea for she will hop on the back of the nearest boat and you will never see her again. Every time I share this idea with a group I have at least an eighth of the hands in a room go up of people wanting to share a story of a young professional who walked out one day—and sometimes for a lunch break or "doctor's appointment"—and just never came back.

DAY 1 — ORIENT AROUND AN ENGAGING TASK FOR THE DAY

While every role—particularly entry-level and service industry ones—have their fair share of inherently mundane tasks (although in chapter 10 I'll show you how to elicit engagement from some of the most unlikely work), day one is not the day to dump them on a young professional new hire. Standing in front of a photocopier for half a day or entering 500 prospects into an Excel spreadsheet is a surefire recipe for the first day to be the last day—of enthusiasm if not also employment. To meet young professionals where they are in their thoughts, hopes, and outright fantasies about the workplace—whether their view of workplace engagement is Ted Mosby on *How I Met Your Mother* or Liz Lemon on *30 Rock*—give them a task that allows them to use their noggin, tap their creativity, and have some FUN (as a reminder that's Full Unadulterated Nonsense). If you're not sure what such a task could be, here are a few examples to jumpstart your own brainstorming:

- Research venues for an upcoming event. Share back findings in a spreadsheet, PowerPoint presentation, or company blog post.

- Share a relevant industry whitepaper and ask for a recommendation of the 2–3 best practices that could be incorporated in your team/department/company.

- Have a young professional sample each appetizer and identify her recommendations for which to feature in a new promotion.

- Use LinkedIn to research prospective partners for a new project.

- Let your young professional partner with other sales associates to create a new window display.

- Take a young professional to an important meeting and give her a specific role in it (even if it's simply listening and documenting particular information).

GIVE TIME TO CUSTOMIZE THE WORKSPACE

DAY 1

Almost nothing gives young professionals a greater sense of satisfaction than having voice in the design of their workspaces. It plays into young professionals' desires for individuality, autonomy, and work-life integration. Let young professionals know what they can and cannot bring and showcase at work prior to their first day. Yes to birthday photos (as long as everyone is fully clothed, there is no evidence of alcohol or substance use, and nobody has inappropriate messages painted on their fingernails). A big resounding no, on the other hand, to painting, breaking down walls, or substituting a desk for a couch (unless you are taking a nod from Zappos, 37Signals, and an increasing number of companies that are shifting from traditional workspaces to more fun, collaborative atmospheres). While the full realization of a workspace may not come for a few weeks—and even then your young professionals will most likely always be adding pictures from company events, new professional and personal awards, and inspirational quotes—you let them start personalizing their space on day one so that they waste no time seeing themselves as permanent residents rather than tourists at your company. Even if an employee's workspace is public, having a small photo of a loved one, a calendar with photos of their favorite tropical islands, or at the very least a name tag with some personalized art sends the equally important message that you are a company that invests in its employees' workplace satisfaction. This is an important ingredient in customer loyalty and for creating a free recruitment channel. When your customers become your employees, it's a win-win for everyone!

As your young professionals assert their identities, values, experiences, and interests in their spaces, make sure that you are taking note of what you see. If an employee is a big fan of *American Idol*, you know to buy them tickets when the newest cast comes through your city. If you see that your young professional is involved with a bunch of social enterprises like Heifer International and Kiva, you can purchase a goat or give a microloan in her name. And if the employee has really been going above and beyond, you encourage her to apply and if accepted, pay for her to go to a professional development program like the StartingBloc Institute for emerging social innovators. Sure, the employee might come back, pack her bags, and start her own social venture turning algae into fuel. More likely than not, if she has enjoyed consistent engagement in her role, built relationships with her colleagues, and received an appropriate level of compensation, she will return and simply be a social intrapreneur within your four walls—spearheading a new employee community involvement program or launching an entirely new department altogether.

LET MICHAEL SCOTT LEAD YOUR OFFICE TOUR

Although I jumped on the bandwagon a few years late, I've been an avid viewer of *The Office* because there is so much to learn about effective workplace management and training from laughing at the mistakes the people on the show make. For those unfamiliar with *The Office*, through April 28, 2011—a sad, sad day in my TV life—Steve Carrell played Michael Scott, a paper company branch manager in Scranton, PA. While I could easily wax on about my favorite episodes—and there are several dozen of them—what's important to know is that Michael Scott is terrible at 99.9 percent of his management functions. Despite his best intentions, he cannot supervise, train, inspire—and have I mentioned—he rarely, if ever, works. But he does one *really* important thing right. He takes the time to know all of his staff and whenever he introduces anyone to them, he gets right to the heart of what makes that person who she is.

Now while I don't recommend announcing your employees' sexual orientations, alcoholism, or infidelities—some of the info Michael regularly reveals to anyone he gives an office tour—I do recommend spending as much time introducing your young professionals to who they will be interacting with as you spend surveying the office space. It's nice to know where the water cooler lives and the code for the restroom. It's even nicer—unless you've spent a lot of time at the water cooler and are now fumbling with the bathroom door—to know who you go to for petty cash, health insurance questions, and ideas for staff service projects. Whether these introductions begin prior to day one or need to wait for the official first day, make sure that they happen. And rather than just announcing "This is Carlos. He's Fiscal Administrative Assistant III," try saying, "This is Carlos. He's been employee of the year the last two years in a row for his role in getting all of our records in order for our big audit. He's your go-to guy for reimbursement requests, and I highly recommend getting on his team at staff development days. He pitches as well as he kicks."

MAKE NICE WITH INFORMATION TECHNOLOGY (IT)

Even if you set your young professionals up with a company email address and network password prior to their first day, inevitably there are going to be tech snafus beyond a direct supervisor's pay grade that require troubleshooting. To save yourself and your young professionals the frustration that grows exponentially each moment that such a glitch is unaddressed, ensure that young professionals are introduced to, have some alone time with, and know how to follow up with the person who handles IT. Coordinate with this person to deliver information about what is an acceptable use of company technology. Can employees check their personal email? Use Facebook, Twitter, or whatever online network is the rage by the time you read this? Can they forward YouTube videos to other staff? Are they allowed and perhaps even encouraged to post to the company blog during workplace hours? What kind of email signature should be attached to their email account?

While I don't recommend having the entire "This is your role. These are your responsibilities" talk on day one, I do recommend dishing about online dos and don'ts, as young professionals will be on their computers engaged in some form of personal communication within a heartbeat, even if it's simply to tell their parents about their first day. I subscribe to the belief that if employees achieve their accountabilities, there is no need for Big Brother-style policies that prevent online and face-to-face nonworkplace related communication. When any employee—but particularly our newest young professionals—feel micromanaged, distrusted, and are prevented from having a little fun in their day, they are more likely to make mistakes, slow down their rate of delivery, disengage, and perhaps outright sabotage.

While I'm certainly not alone in my beliefs, I recognize that there are individuals and organizations that simply don't want an employee engaging in non-work-related communication. Set your young professional up for success by being transparent about the use of online computers. If you have filters preventing or tracking certain forms of communication, let them know. And if you are in a role where you get to shape policies, ensure that there is a reason for the rules you are making and upholding. Young professionals can be your greatest online proselytizers—bringing what goes on within your four walls to existing and new clients and customers. Through their individual and group blogging networks such as Brazen Careerist or 20 Something Bloggers, they also can attract talent your way. If you are scared of what they might be saying, perhaps it's time to ask why you are hiring and growing talent that has something negative to say. Are you not filtering out negative new hires in your recruitment and hiring process? Or does your young talent have something negative to say because of what your company is or isn't doing that it's time for you to address?

SET UP A LUNCH DATE

DAY 1

While seasoned employees may not give lunch much thought, and sometimes work right through it—for new young professionals, particularly on their first day—it is the most important hour of the day. It can assuage any lingering fears about fit if new employees connect with fellow staff. It can just as easily magnify them if they have a negative experience—if they feel like an outsider in conversations, learn too many downsides to the job or staff, or worse yet, if they wind up eating alone.

If the direct supervisor is close in age with new hires, will be working very closely with them, or if they just have great chemistry, a one-on-one date will be fine. Another idea I recommend for making that first lunch the right kind of memorable is setting up a group date with other young professionals, much like our hypothetical manager Chris did. You don't need to script it like a date on *The Bachelor* or *The Bachelorette*, although you can meet with more seasoned young professionals in advance and give them some recommended speaking points: what their first 90 days looked like, fun company traditions and rituals, and if or how employees get together outside of work. If appropriate, you can also equip them with questions to ask new hires, such as:

- How has your first day been going so far?

- What attracted you to Bradley's Books?

- What questions are lurking that would be more comfortable to ask us than your supervisor?

- We are getting together for an informal happy hour on Friday. Want to join us?

While the direct manager can check in both with the new hire and the other young professionals after lunch to see how the matchmaking went, this is one of the few times I encourage you to hold back and not ask a lot of questions. It's important for young employees to have a rich peer group at work and the space to have conversations without worrying there is a bug in the wall.

GET TO RELATIONSHIP BUILDING

The most important relationship for young professionals to build is their relationship with their direct supervisor or manager. Even if you opt out of first day lunch so that young professionals can "date" fellow staff without feeling like ma or pa is chaperoning, carve out time to gab. Be curious, and ask your new hires what gets them jazzed. Begin to explore how they like to work and what they need to be successful. Discover what they like to do for fun and how you can support them to get the most out of their employment.

Just as importantly, let a new employee get to know you—your professional and personal interests, preferred working style, and any best practices you have developed that have made you successful in your role. Show that you are someone who is equally accessible for questions about the mundane—*What's the best snack food in the vending machine?*—to the more significant—*How do you deal with Kurt in corporate when he shares way too much personal information and makes you feel uncomfortable?* In the next chapter you will explore the specific kinds of information young professionals need to know to be self-directed. But even on day one, you can start building the rapport that young professionals hunger for with their leaders.

SCHEDULE A QUICK DATE WITH HR

Even if you arm young professionals with a virtual orientation experience they complete prior to their first day, it's important for them to still have contact with HR when they start. A downside to having one of a new employee's first touches with a company be virtual is that employees may have questions that go unanswered or not have a relationship established with HR should questions or concerns come up down the line.

When a new employee meets with HR, it should be clear exactly who in the department handles each of its myriad issues. Who is the person that will be hounding the employee if any documents are missing from the personnel file? Who handles employee medical insurance and sick leave? Pension programs and vacation requests? The all-important payroll? If policies and procedures governing these areas—as well as the equally important and often overlooked (until a problem arises) spheres of company ethics and security—are not online, make sure that HR succinctly covers and then gives the new hire the necessary paperwork and handbook outlining them. Frame the discussion not only in terms of compliance—which will be easy for young professionals to tune out—but also around the perks of the job. For example:

- What are employee health benefits? What *exactly* is and isn't covered?

- How much vacation, sick, and personal time is provided? How does this grow with each year of employment?

- Does the company provide any kind flexible scheduling? For whom? How does one take advantage of it?

- What kind of retirement plans does the company offer? How do employer contributions shift the longer an employee is with a company? What should an employee do to maximize savings? (Remember, most young professionals have no idea the difference between a 401(k) and a 403(b). They just know that their parents lost much of their savings from their employers as they were seeking to retire. Help them to help themselves.)

Also, if you are a direct supervisor, please know the policies yourself. While you by no means need to be able to recite each verbatim, you should understand them enough so that you can answer questions, reinforce rules, and know when and to whom you refer to in HR in situations that do arise.

ADDRESS LINGERING ANXIETY

DAY 1

As one of my favorite self-help authors Susan Jeffers preaches—you've got to feel your fear, and take action anyway. To have the courage to do so, however, necessitates knowing when the payoff of not taking action is finally greater than the discomfort of staying grounded in the familiarity of the existing fear. In other words, for young professionals to get to the other side of feeling like a somewhat lost newbie to a place where they are integrated into your workplace and driving results, they need to know the importance of speaking up. Let them know that staying quiet and flying under the radar will make them more uncomfortable and less successful in the long run than coming clean about what they don't know or understand and what current or future worries are gnawing away at them.

Veteran employees can assuage anxiety by initiating conversations with "I remember when I first started, I felt _____," "If you're anything like me, you are probably feeling _____" or my favorite "Know that the only stupid question is the question that you keep asking yourself but nobody else." Direct supervisors should ask specifically what if anything a new hire is curious about on day one and make clear that they are available if and when questions about roles, responsibilities, policies, or the company itself emerge. Then, because our actions project louder than our words, identify moments when young employees look like a deer in headlights to see if you can be of service. Just as importantly, show that asking questions is not merely for the young and the new. If you are unsure of something or a situation simply rubs you the wrong way, model courageous communication by opening your mouth and addressing the discomfort.

INTRODUCE THE FOCUS FOR THE WEEK

To transfer a successful first day into a successful first week, make sure that young professionals leave day one knowing what they will tackle when they show up for day two. Rather than giving them a to-do list of one-off tasks to move through, I recommend giving them a couple of discrete and measurable goals to achieve by the end of the week. Then, together with your new hire, work backward from where you want the young professional to be by the end of the first week to where she is by the end of day one to see the specific action steps that should be undertaken to achieve success.

Let's imagine that you are a manager, Molly, in a PR firm that represents small business owners looking to get their message out in front of a larger community audience. Your new hire, Serjik, is going to be a social media specialist—responsible for getting your clients more face time on Facebook and Twitter. It's a new area and you are almost as unsure as Serjik of where to start, but you're digging this whole streamlined week one focus idea and are ready to give it a whirl. Here's how—in broad strokes—you can dive in.

PR Manager Molly Identifies the Week One Focus With Social Media Specialist Serjik

Molly: I imagine it can feel a little overwhelming to spearhead a new project and I want you to be able to get to know our clients before having to show up with an action plan.

Serjik: Thanks. I have a lot of ideas, but I also feel like I have a lot to learn before I'm set loose.

Molly: In order to know what's working as well as what isn't, by next week I'd like to have you report back on each of our 18 clients' social media presences. What does each look like? Who—people and companies—are interacting with them? What messages are, and aren't, getting traction?

Serjik: That sounds awesome. You're actually giving me permission to hang out online.

Molly: Yes. Sort of. Let's talk about what "hanging out" should look like in order to have as complete of a report as I'd like.

Serjik: Of course. Are those the main questions you want me to address—what each presence looks like, the kinds of people who are engaging, and the messages that are eliciting the most engagement?

Molly: Exactly. I'd like to have you create a one page report for each client with a one to two paragraph summary answering each of those questions, as well as five-ish specific examples from the online messages. This will be a great resource for us as well as for the clients themselves.

Serjik: Okay. I'm with you so far.

Molly: In order for you to have the report to share back next Tuesday, I'd like to hear where you plan to be Monday, Friday, and each day before going backward to tomorrow when you come in. I believe that working backward is one of the best ways to ensure that time is allocated toward taking steps in the order necessary to achieve a goal.

Serjik: Makes sense to me. So by next Monday I'd like to have the report essentially written. I'll do some editing, maybe swap out some examples and add anything that I've observed in the final day that I think is relevant. That means this Thursday and Friday I need to be writing. I anticipate it will take me both days both to write up the 18 clients and keep observing. Especially on Twitter, Friday tends to be an active day. Which means, yikes, tomorrow is really about tracking each client once an hour to see what if anything is said and making notes, starting to write down examples, because then I need to start writing. And I imagine you're going to have other stuff for me as well.

Molly: I will, but this really is the priority. Your plan sounds great to me. Know that I'm here if you want to run anything by me, but I want to stay out of your way as much as possible and let you do your thing.

When managers get young professionals clear that success is measured by results delivered and have them see that each choice they make needs to build upon the last to move them—and a project—from desire to achievement, they develop one of the most important habits any employee can develop. While longer term or repetitive goals may not always so neatly break down this way, initially managers should give a focus that can be. Resist the desire to jump in and tell young professionals what to do moment to moment, unless a mistake is about to be or has been made that needs to be immediately addressed. Instead, observe young professionals' ability to work backward without overlooking key steps. Make note of where they are successful following through with their plan, troubleshooting any hiccups that arise on the path to completion, and staying focused amidst the distractions that inevitably come up. A keen manager can use these observations in the days to come to determine how best to inspire top-notch performance, give the right balance of structure and freedom, and provide ongoing feedback and design probationary goals. Managers should assign work in the first days of employment where there can be some snafus in order for young professionals—and them—to learn how best to rock 'n' roll with one another moving forward. A little failure is okay—as long as it's an opportunity to learn and grow.

As you tweak or perhaps even scrap and redesign your day one experience for your young professionals—and hopefully keep the tactics that have cross-generational appeal for all of your new hires!—strive to create a genuine balance between structure and freedom. While you want there to be breath in that first day, you also want your new employees, particularly those who might be starting their first full-time job with you, to feel comfortable and supported. For this generation, that means knowing how to focus their time, feeling a part of a community, and getting to tap the creativity so many have been lauded for.

Tweet-Sized Takeaways

- **Put your policies and procedures into a hip virtual experience for young professionals to view at home prior to day one.**

- **Let young professionals know what to expect on day one and how (and how *not*) to show up.**

- **Show young professionals the best of their future work by assigning an engaging day one task.**

- Make young professionals comfortable in their new digs. Have them customize their workspace and get a lay of the land—and the people in it.

- Get young professionals full computer access. Ensure they know company online policies, and that the policies drive the results you seek.

- Set young professionals up on a mutually beneficial lunch date.

- The most important relationship for young professionals to build is with their direct supervisor or manager. Start day one.

- Ensure young professionals have ongoing virtual or paper access to company policies, procedures, and perks.

- Encourage new hires to name their fear(s) and diffuse them with clarification, support, and an open door policy.

- Identify where you want young professionals to be by the end of their first week. Show them how to work backward to illuminate the steps to get there.

chapter 3

Give Them What They Need to Know to Succeed

"The leader lays down the melody line and encourages individual band members to improvise around them."

Bradley Porten

I think it is pretty safe to say that you want your young professionals to be successful. And I hope we're still on the same page when I say that you don't mind an initial investment of time and energy in an employee as long as you get what you put in down the line. Where onboarding gets a little divisive is in the implementation of the invested time and energy. Your employee's first few days go by, and for the majority of companies there is an implicit sense—or at least a deeply desired wish—for new hires to be self-sufficient and ready to play with the big kids.

Your young professionals need a lot more than what you can give them in a one-off orientation or a welcome packet in order to perform their roles to the level of excellence I hope you expect. They need to know from their managers as concretely as they can give it to them exactly what success looks like—how it will be measured and what they should do to achieve it—as well as have access to the resources to make it happen. The payoff for doing it right the first time, of course, is to not have to continually invest in doing it.

 ## ARTICULATE ROLE RESPONSIBILITIES CLEARLY AND CREATE ACCOUNTABILITY

Remember in the intro how we talked about the far-reaching impact of your young professionals spending more years in school than any previous generation? Well, add the generation's predilection to seeing a syllabus as a holy book as yet one more result. Giving your new hires a tangible, go-to reminder of what you expect them to do is important if you want to be on the same page about accountability and have a means for assessment, salary discussions, and promotion. It also enables a manager to make recommendations for training and development. While HR most likely put together some kind of job description to advertise a position, do not assume it spells out what a direct supervisor believes are the most important role responsibilities, or that a sense of accountability is implicit within it.

I love HR—really I do—so if that is your function please don't slam the book and use it to swat bugs. I speak what I see. And these eyes have seen too many job descriptions used to recruit and screen candidates that fail to comprehensively capture what the role actually entails once someone is in it. It also often fails to describe what a supervisor for the person in that role expects and why. This is a bummer for young professionals, their supervisors, and ultimately HR, who is forced to recruit yet again for an unsuccessfully filled position.

 ## Responsibilities Vs. Accountabilities

While these two words often get used interchangeably, as Roger Connors, Tom Smith, and Craig Hickman, the authors of *The Oz Principle* explain, "Responsibility may be bestowed, but accountability must be taken." Somebody may be responsible for something, but that does not guarantee she feels a sense of accountability to make it happen.

 Role **responsibilities** are the specific, repeatable tasks that an employee must perform to achieve success in a role.

For example: Tabulate online purchases in ClientBuy system for weekly department meeting; Recruit a minimum of 50 prospective medical assistants to each quarterly open house. In addition to giving a document identifying these responsibilities, supervisors need to talk through them with employees and explain how to prioritize them. Some of the most common responsibilities for a young new hire in an office pretty irrespective of role include: **communicating, tracking, reporting, maintaining, repairing, monitoring,** and with increasing responsibility in a position, you will most likely find **developing, budgeting, managing,** and **evaluating**. When you list and describe responsibilities, it's important to include the **what, how, for whom,** and **when**.

 Accountabilities are created from the why that motivates a person's responsibilities. It is your secret weapon for engagement and follow-through. When employees understand the significance of fulfilling each of their responsibilities—how they affect the customer or client, the company, department, supervisor, themselves—then you are setting that young professional up to get them done.

Let's return to the example of a new hire for a medical assistant training program. If I'm in that role, first I get clear that I need to bring 50 people into a room at each open house. That's my responsibility. I need a good *why* in order for accountability to take place. If you can tell me that the performance goal—which we will investigate in more depth throughout the book—is to get 15 new students each quarter and that we have a 30 percent sign-up rate from our open houses, then suddenly I understand the importance of that number 50.

 ## SHARE COMPANY VISION, MISSION, AND CORE VALUES AGAIN AND AGAIN

Whether verbatim or in your own words, can you—right now—articulate your company's vision, mission, and core values? If you are like the majority of employees and executives, I'm going to wager "no."

 ### Vision Vs. Mission Vs. Core Values

An organization's **vision** identifies where it is headed. The **mission** is the specific way the company moves toward the vision. And the organization's **core values** are the attitudes, beliefs, and practices that make the vision and mission a reality.

Companies whose employees have a clear sense of vision, mission, and core values enjoy higher profits, more engaged employees, and greater innovation. I'm always amused when a company asks to bring me in to develop their vision and mission statement and to help identify core values. For while verbiage that connects with employees is important, what trumps copywriting is a continual plan for how to connect employees back to these backbones of company culture. Rather than investing hours and dollars in coming up with good speak, I'd love to see more organizations work with consultants to devise an ongoing plan for how to engage employees in living the vision, mission, and values. It is important to share what you've got in these areas with young professionals when they begin. After all, this is the first generation of employees who can articulate their own core values—contribution, learning, growth, family, and work-life integration—usually from the moment they walk in your door. They are deeply attracted to "who" a company is—its soul—and what it does in and outside its four walls. It's even more important, though, for companies to engage young professionals in seeing how through their own learning, growth, and contribution—yes, please use young professionals' values to hook them into yours—they can uphold their company's vision, enact its mission, honor its values, feel a part of a workplace family, and play a role in redefining any of these culture pieces should they become outdated and in need of some tweaking. This is what will facilitate lasting investment, greater performance, and lasting retention for the right employees.

Perhaps the most famous company to orient its prospective and new employees in company values is also headquartered in my community: Zappos. On its recruitment page, Zappos asks prospects to make sure the company's core values reflect who they are before applying. To this end, every candidate called for an interview meets with a hiring manager to discuss skills, experiences, and role requirements. If they pass this round of screening, candidates also meet with HR to see if they are a culture fit with the organization. As CEO Tony Hsieh proudly asserts, Zappos hires—and on occasion, fires—based on employee alignment with core values.

When hired, every new Zappos employee goes through an intensive, four-week training program that covers the company's history, what it means to be a service-driven organization, the long-term vision, and most importantly, how Zappos lives its values within its walls. As employee Melissa L. illustrates in a post on the company's employee blog, during the next phase of onboarding—the transition from the initial training program to the company floor, known as "incubation"—customer loyalty personnel are still encouraged to root themselves in the "who" of the company. The incubation team playfully immerses new hires in exploring each core value by making learning fun and interactive. For example, to explore the company value of "Deliver Wow Through Service," the team leads participants through Zappos Zamily Zeud. Rather than browbeating employees with content or asking them to regurgitate it in a quiz, they let their young new hires get it into their bones through a friendly, community-building competition. Jennifer Rios, who has gone through the program, believes it not only showed her how to live the core value while at work, but also to make it a part of who she is in her daily life, showing greater gratitude to the people who provide her with service.

 ## REVEAL COMPANY AND TEAM SHORT- AND LONG-TERM GOALS

If you want your young professionals to stay invested in their work, it's essential they understand what that work is and where it's headed. Let your new hires know approximately halfway through their first month exactly what your organization has on tap over the next 90 days. Are you finishing up a big internal audit? Getting ready to launch a new program? Opening your first international office? Even if company goals seem completely unrelated to your employee's role—for example, your young professional is a customer service representative and your company is mid-search for a new COO—inviting young professionals into the 411 of your company will make them feel valued, trusted, and a part of something larger than themselves. In addition to keeping young professionals abreast of short-term company aims, let them know where your company is headed more long-term, by which I mean two to five years down the line. This supports them to transfer this kind of long-term thinking to both their work and career development within your four walls.

Remember that withholding information—even if you think you are protecting employees from frightening or disappointing information—rarely works. Employees, particularly young professionals who are used to being in-the-know, just get distrustful when they sniff out secrecy. And when they inevitably trace the smell back to the source and unearth that layoffs, takeovers, or relocations are on the horizon and this was hidden from them, they feel deceived rather than protected. While I hope that you are not bringing young professionals into a company unraveling into crisis, identify what you can tell your new hires about where you are headed organizationally, even when the outlook is glum. And most importantly, be transparent about where opportunities lie—even if up close everything on the horizon appears shrouded by obstacles. This will boost morale, productivity, and may trigger innovation that directs your department back on the path to success.

FOCUS TRAINING ON WHAT'S RELEVANT

DAY 1

It's easy, particularly in a company with a formal training department, to see training—much like orientation—as a one or two day endeavor where a manager sends new employees to get "trained." But what does "trained" actually look like? And why might the notion of leaving one's office to get "trained" be inherently flawed?

For the last two years I have been on my local ASTD chapter's board, so know that I'm not suggesting that training is an ineffective investment of money, time, or resources. However, when experts in developing human capital like KnowledgeAdvisors suggest that approximately 60 percent of training does not get implemented, I hope a red flag shoots up for you. If a young professional's direct manager is not a part of influencing the content and the skills being engendered in that training—and even more importantly solidifying that training once that young professional returns—well, then yes, training in this case is going to be an ineffective investment of money, time, and resources. It takes approximately those 90 days I keep rattling on about to create or reshape and solidify a habit. While I believe I can train anyone to be a compelling presenter or an effective coach, I know that I cannot do that in a few days nor can I do that if the person I'm training does not have daily opportunities to water the seed that we planted.

Fortunately, there is a lot of literature in the learning and development world about how to ensure training is an ongoing process that engenders the results that are sought. For our purposes, I want you to identify the specific skills, behaviors, and knowledge that you want your young professionals to demonstrate by the end of their first 90 days.

Next, ask yourself how you will know if this acquisition has been achieved?

Then, spend some time working backward from week to week until you rewind to the first day. This will ensure that you give your young new hire the time and direction to develop everything you have identified you will be looking for as an indicator of success.

At what points do you need to be teaching new content? When are you allowing for it to be tried out and refined? At what points do you bring in an expert trainer?

Once you have identified what you need to set your young professionals up to be successful, compare the training that currently exists—formal (actual classes in such areas as customer service or sexual harassment) and informal (moment to moment role coaching). What is serving your goals? What is not? And if your young professionals' success is in any way linked to your own, what will be the payoff for committing to the necessary tweaks you are identifying?

BE PROACTIVE AND TEACH YOUNG PROFESSIONALS INTEGRAL SYSTEMS AND PROCEDURES

This is one of the least exciting parts of onboarding any employee, particularly young professionals who may not have gone through it with a former employer. They need more hand-holding than more seasoned employees. Most likely they will need more reminders when they forget how to complete a particular task, or give it a go on their own and it's got some...area for growth. There are policies guiding every aspect of work—dress, behavior, benefits, grievances—but since we're focusing on setting young professionals up to be successful in their roles in this chapter, I'm focusing on the systems and procedures regarding the actual work your young professionals are charged with doing.

Systems Vs. Procedures

Systems are the ways of completing work while **procedures** are the steps involved in mastering the system.

If you are a manager, you may never have thought about or compiled a list of them, particularly if you are a smaller company where everyone has more freedom in how they complete their work. Yet as I've said before and I'll say again, your young professionals need an appropriate balance of structure and freedom. While giving them license to be creative in how they approach a presentation can be a good thing, neglecting to give step-by-step instructions for how to fill out an expense report—not so much.

Managers want to review the major responsibilities for a young professional's role and compile a list of each of the tasks that young professional will need to complete. Then, identify the systems and corresponding procedures that inform each of these tasks. This part can be subjective. As a manager you may have previously been in the role or supervised others in it who have a very specific way of completing one or more of its elements. If it's integral to the role, you absolutely want to develop step-by-step instructions for it. In the example of the expense report, teach employees to download the form from the company server; record their name, the department, and project; summarize the event by expense and vendor; attach all receipts and an attendee list; have direct supervisor and department manager sign off; make a photocopy for your records; submit to Carlos (and drop a hint about teaming up on the next staff development day). You are smart. You picked up my book, after all, so you get the idea.

On the other hand, if you simply know that there's a best practice that can be used, share this. Then let go of any attachment to having your young professionals use it. As human nature will have it, the more you give suggestions as gifts rather than as requirements, the more likely it is that your young professionals will embrace them.

EXPLAIN THE CHAIN OF COMMAND

DAY 7

I pride myself on rarely losing my levelheadedness professionally, but I once went "worst manager ever" on a summer intern, who I will call Andy. And—I'm so red in the face remembering the incident—it was his first day. I had given him what I thought was a pretty spectacular office tour (ripe with what I considered the right balance of cheekiness and professionalism) just before I headed out for lunch. (Rest assured, he was going to take lunch with the other summer interns once I returned!) I gave him clear, step-by-step instructions for how to enter some basic data for a report I needed to present that afternoon. So I was pretty surprised when I returned to my office after a quick bite, and there was no Andy.

I popped into the neighboring offices to see if anybody had seen him. "I think Andy went to the bathroom," one person reported. "Maybe he decided to go to lunch a little early," another person offered. Finally, someone suggested he might have needed to present his driver's license to HR because he didn't have it with him when he filled out his initial paperwork. I headed across the floor to HR. "He was here," they informed me. "But he left fifteen minutes ago."

Beginning to think that maybe Andy was abducted by aliens, I decided to walk down the hallway to hunt for him, and I saw he was sitting in another office. The office of the Executive Director. I shamefully took a step back against the wall before I could be detected, pulled out my phone and pretended to be checking email, while I probably not so inconspicuously in retrospect placed my ear against the wall and listened in. I heard Andy talking about his last semester's classes and his travel plans for the summer. Yes, apparently Andy had no problem confiding in the ED that he was planning to go backpacking for a week during his first month of an eight-week internship. Before I vomited in my mouth, I made my way back to the office and prepared my tirade I would never repeat to anyone (except to poor Andy) once he came back to my office. This wasn't for another thirty minutes—five minutes prior to his lunch break. And as I'm sure you can imagine, my request for the time sensitive data entry was never answered.

Your young professionals are used to an overly casual relationship with their parents, and in most cases, their friends' parents. This has translated into many young people entering the workplace thinking, like Andy, that it's okay to stop by and chat up senior leaders with a new idea or simply for small talk. As Andy shared in his defense, "When you introduced me during the office tour she said stop by anytime."

Making Andy wrong didn't serve either of us very well. He never came back after his backpacking trip, and most of the other interns scowled at me over the course of the summer. Even as someone less than half a decade older than them—a fellow member of their generation—I had made a monumental mistake. I had failed to address our chain of command.

This is one of those onboarding practices that is so easy to overlook. Yet doing it takes anywhere from five minutes to an hour max, supposing you've got a really large company and your young professional interfaces with a lot of different staff. Take the time to go through the company directory. Let young professionals know who they should contact and for what purposes. When you know, share how that person likes to be communicated with. *Drop by Sandy's office ONLY if you don't first get a response from Cassie. Sandy never picks up the phone and hates interoffice email.* Similarly, teach young professionals how to refer to senior leaders and what is and isn't appropriate to say to them. My ED had a terrific policy of wanting everyone to call her by her initials, and it made her more accessible. But while I never did find out, I suspect that despite her informality she still didn't want interns dropping into her office unscheduled to give her a college year-in-review or summer itinerary catch-up.

BE TRANSPARENT ABOUT THE PROMOTION CHANNEL

DAY 14

Most likely you have at some point encountered the stereotype that the current generation of young professionals has their eyes set on supervisory and sometimes even senior leadership roles by the end of their first day on the job. It's true. In a culture where even kindergarten classrooms have class presidents, your youngest workers have been immersed in leadership talk most of their lives. And many of them have significant leadership experience. Whether they have served as mayor like Tashua Allman, John Tyler Hammons, or Matt Delligatti (three of over one dozen current twentysomething mayors), launched a tech startup out of their college dorm room a la Mark Zuckerberg, or perhaps been a little less ambitious and simply founded and run a community nonprofit organization like yours truly, by the time they are leaving college, many so-called entry-level professionals have had more experience overseeing a company or significant project and inspiring or managing staff and volunteers than their supervisors.

Does this mean young professionals are entitled to a promotion after their first 90 days? No. I don't believe anyone is entitled to much of anything beyond their basic human rights. But chastising young professionals for their leadership drive—publicly or privately—serves nobody. When 80 million Baby Boomers retire over the next decade and companies are left with just over 40 million members of Generation X to fill their roles, remember it is our young professionals who will be stepping into leadership positions, in many cases earlier than in any other generation of workers. When you recognize the leadership potential many of them come to you with, be it dormant or very much in your face, and you let your young professionals know how they can position themselves for upward mobility, you tap into their values and desires. You usually give a nice jolt to their engagement. And when your top young talent gets approached by one of your competitors, you more than likely retain them.

Letting young professionals know about a company's promotion pathway should be a straightforward and ongoing conversation. At approximately two weeks into employment, introduce the possibilities for growth in your company. And don't be surprised if they initiate the conversation even before you do. Let them know about opportunities directly above them as well as those that might be lateral: performing similar work in a different department or on a different project. Explain who makes decisions about promotions and set them up to be selected for one by letting them know the criteria. Wouldn't it be great to be seen as the developer of top talent in your company? And even if some of your young professionals get passed over, think about how their performance will increase if they know eyes are on them for future possibilities.

 ## CO-CREATE A CAREER DEVELOPMENT PLAN

My soul sister in onboarding young professionals, Emily Bennington, believes that every young professional should complete a career development plan within her first two weeks. For as Emily says, "the onboarding process is about two things: *technical career support*—giving new employees the tools to do their jobs successfully—and emotional engagement—helping them become invested in your organization. If handled correctly, the career development plan achieves both."

 A **career development** plan, at its core, is the action plan for how a young professional will carry out her role responsibilities.

A career development plan need not be a complicated process. It's a co-creation between employee, direct supervisor, and team manager or mentor—should those roles exist. The supervisor identifies the areas that are most important to an employee's job function—the chief responsibilities. The employee can then take the lead on identifying specific, measurable action steps she will take to achieve them. Supervisors, team managers, or mentors can of course weigh in, but your most important role will be what happens moving forward—providing the training, support, feedback, and accountability for the employee to realize the plan.

As Emily cautions, more important than getting the plan right is to get it *done*. "It's a breathing document that can be altered at any time." The plan should also be revisited every 90 days, so that a new plan can be created for the next quarter. It should also be referred to whenever you are providing feedback or coaching. For Emily, not having a career development plan is what—much like me—sparked her obsession to study companies and young professionals who have been set up to succeed.

A Sneak Peak At Emily's Story (In Her Own Words)

I started my career working for a very small marketing agency with fewer than 10 employees. In one sense, this was an excellent experience. Without the luxury of support staff and with minimal resources, I learned very early how to think for myself, multitask effectively, and do whatever it takes to get the job done. I didn't have any kind of formal onboarding or training so it was very much baptism-by-fire. I left the agency after a few years and took a job as advertising director for a regional lifestyle magazine—and it was the same thing. On my first day at the magazine, the editor-in-chief literally handed me a stack of sales kits and wished me luck. I knew nothing about the magazine's readership, circulation numbers, or which businesses had already been approached and the status of those relationships. So there I was, about to go on the road as a representative of the magazine to potential clients—and I didn't know anything about it! Before long, the excitement of having a new challenge dissolved into frustration and I left. I wrote *Effective Immediately* and began preaching about onboarding because I want to give new hires the early career support I never had. I want companies to understand that it's in their long-term best interest to provide it.

HAVE YOUNG PROFESSIONALS IDENTIFY THEIR SWOT

DAY 30

One strategy I recommend that anyone looking to strategize for career success use is a personal SWOT (Strengths, Weaknesses, Opportunities, and Threats) analysis. This enables someone to take an entrepreneurial approach to her career development and get clear on how she can create and attract the right opportunities her way. By recognizing where and how you play best, where you are not so strong, the opportunities you have and can create for yourself, and the likely as well as unforeseen threats that might get in your way, you make yourself responsible for your own career development and engage in discovery that is inherently actionable. I highly recommend making a personal SWOT analysis a part of your career development planning with your employees—particularly young professionals who, as you have learned, are eager to learn and grow and ascend up your organizational ladder.

Once a young professional has completed a personal SWOT, the most important thing her manager can do is help her apply her insight to future short- and long-term goal setting. My favorite questions to facilitate this kind of self-reflection and corresponding action include:

- Where is it most important for you to focus your attention over the next 90 days so that you are playing to your strengths 70–80 percent of your time and your weaknesses no more than 20–30 percent?

- Which two to three strengths and one to two weaknesses will be most important for you to grow based on what you've discovered about opportunities and threats?

- How will you take personal responsibility for your success by capitalizing on anticipated opportunities and protecting yourself against likely and unforeseen threats?

PROVIDE RELEVANT CONTACT INFORMATION

Let's end this chapter on one of, if not the easiest, tactics to put into practice.

Make sure young professionals exit their first week armed with contact info for all of the key people they will need to reach: fellow employees, clients/customers, key stakeholders, previous staff (if they have agreed to provide support if initially needed), and prospects (if appropriate). Despite our online information age, too many professionals—particularly the youngest ones—compromise their efficiency by having to search for contact information online or through previous employees' scribbled notes. Nothing encourages young professionals to distract themselves like having to be online hunting down contact info. Managers must keep records independent of their individual employees' contact files so that new employees can connect with the people they need to connect with as soon as they come on to the job. I recommend providing them with phone numbers, email addresses, office locations (whether that is physical addresses or site/room information for your company's employees), as well as social media contacts, if that's appropriate.

It's easy to get stuck thinking about what's missing from your company's onboarding program. Or to beat yourself up over areas you have mistakenly glossed over when bringing on new young professionals. Remember, you don't set future new hires up for success by getting stuck on your own or others' past shortcomings. As you hopefully have discovered in this chapter, most of the tactics for setting young professionals up to succeed during their first days and weeks with a company are as much about initiating conversations as they are about committing to continue them.

When young professional Hanna Tadesse began her first post-college marketing role with the consulting firm Syska Hennessy, she says that her supervisor and future mentor, Mary Moore, gave her the information she needed to be successful. Most importantly,

Mary did not bombard Hanna with too many directives. "We got together every week for coffee and Mary always had an open door policy. She explained my responsibilities to me in phases throughout my first 90 days. I wasn't expected to learn everything in the first day or week. Mary understood that I would excel more by not having pressure put on me." As *you* think about the tactics you have just encountered, what is most important for you to start applying in your onboarding? How can *you* give your young professionals what they need to know in a way that sets them up to succeed and honors their learning curve?

Tweet-Sized Takeaways

- Articulate role responsibilities clearly and explain their significance in fostering employee accountability.

- Connect young professionals to the *who* of your organization through consistent engagement with vision, mission, and values.

- Be transparent about where your team and company are headed in the short and long term.

- Provide ongoing training to develop the real skills, behaviors, and content required for young professional success.

- Educate young professionals step-by-step in how to complete their core work responsibilities.

- Identify the people young employees need to contact and appropriate decorum for interactions.

- Let young employees know the myriad ways they can advance in your company.

- Support young employees to create a personalized career development plan for them to achieve their goals.

- As a discrete and actionable component of career planning, have young professionals create a personal SWOT analysis.

- Give new employees full contact information for anyone you anticipate they will need to contact.

chapter 4

Integrate Them Into Your Workplace Culture

"If you get the culture right then most
of the other stuff will happen naturally."

Tony Hsieh

Although the women in my family are notorious for butchering common proverbs—
I'm pretty sure my grandma once said, "A bird in the hand gathers no moss"—I'm going
to defy my upbringing and use one that is constructive for framing the relationship
between your young professionals and your goal of 90-day onboarding success. "Hitch
your wagon to a star." Your wagon is your young professional and your star is your
company culture. If for any reason that image doesn't work for you, simply recognize that

getting your young professionals incorporated in your culture should be one of your top onboarding goals. For when you honor young professionals' desire to be a valued member of a workplace community, what they offer that community and what they receive from it will be mutually beneficial.

Young professionals don't like to draw rigid boundaries between work and life. In case you have forgotten, recall for a moment that young professionals actually laugh a bit at the notion of work-life balance. This is significant not only because young professionals are typically self-aware enough not to strive for a kind of balance that is elusive, but also because they don't want the kind of balance that preceding generations have chased in the first place. Tiffany Monhollon, a marketing and corporate communications professional expresses the reason well, saying that while work-life balance is nice in theory, "Every day has all this possibility, and my ideas are virtually endless… so even given all the time in the world, still, there wouldn't be enough time to get it all done. I am the kind of person who always wants to be moving, exploring, learning, growing." For many young professionals like Tiffany, the goal is not to work less. It's to do more increasingly responsible, engaging, and impactful work in a community of like-minded people.

Most young professionals want work and life to be interconnected. They hunger to work for a company that feels like a natural extension of their own personal brand. If a young professional values creativity and risk taking, she wants her company to engender these qualities in its staff. If she gives 10 percent of her income to philanthropic causes, she wants her company to invest 10 percent of its profits the same way. An attractive company culture is to a young professional what honey is to a bee. So if your goal is keeping your young new hires on track for success at the end of their first quarter, invest the time, energy, and resources in a yummy honey recipe.

HOOK YOUNG PROFESSIONALS INTO UNIQUE CULTURAL FEATURES

After about two months, just as your young professionals are getting the swing of things and the novelty of your company and their role in it is starting to wane, stimulate their continued investment by getting them involved in and excited by your company's traditions and rituals. Some elements of your culture will be immediately apparent. For example, young professionals at Google's headquarters in Mountain View, CA—affectionately referred to as Googleplex—need only wander the halls to see massage chairs, a pool table, or a piano. Other facets of your culture, however, may need a little more unearthing—or in some cases, developing. One of the easiest ways to get your young professionals involved in your culture is to have them share their experiences with it. Whether it's writing testimonials for your Facebook fan page or employee blog, documenting colleagues at work (and hopefully sometimes at play!) for company events, or having them share their candid experiences with prospective new hires, when employees have the opportunity to reflect on the culture they will take more of an active role in it.

Sodexo has done a keen job over the last few years of taking itself from "the biggest company nobody had ever heard of," as they say, to an in-demand employer for recent grads through promoting its culture online. Their secret weapon is their brand ambassadors. Sodexo's talent acquisition team has done a stunning job of onboarding their brand ambassadors—a combination of recruiters, hiring managers, and other members of HR—to light it up on social media. They post messages and read and respond to questions and chats on LinkedIn and Facebook from Sodexo candidates. They provide content on the company and share their firsthand experiences on Sodexo's career blog. They even use Sodexo-related Twitter handles to tweet. For example, from @SodexoAmy: "R U a Chef looking for a gr8 next career step? Chk out a new culinary site #jobs #food #chefs #Sodexo http://t.co/EBnOOVg." According to Sherie Valderamma, Sodexo's senior director of talent acquisition, Sodexo has never had an employee misuse social media. The key is providing a lot of training for reasons why Sodexo is using social media to build its employer brand, the strategies for engaging with potential candidates, differentiating between what to respond to and what to pass off, and providing periodic refreshers.

But perhaps your company has a strict policy on employees talking about their work experiences—even the good ones. I was incredibly surprised how many young professionals who love their companies were prevented from sharing their positive onboarding experiences with me for this book. Even when legal means well, sometimes they feel no proselytizing about a company is better than a few naysayers. I respectfully disagree, but it is what it is. So here are four simple, cheap, and effective ways to engage your young professional in your culture beyond taking to social media:

- Develop a company vision board adorned with inspirational quotes, pictures, and company goals.

- Support a culture of appreciation by creating a gratitude wall. When the impulse strikes, employees can post who and what they are grateful for.

- Create a mini library of books—which can be used/donated if on a budget— that are relevant to your employees. In addition to typical business and management titles, make sure to include books on self-improvement and career development.

- Create a culture task force—and make sure your young professionals are on it! Charge the group to make actionable recommendations that are specific to your company.

Companies with an "employees first" ethos invest in their company cultures. As a result, they effortlessly attract young talent and keep them hooked through simple, ongoing traditions like posting baby photos of employees at Facebook, or dressing up on Halloween and throwing an all-day extravaganza like Southwest Airlines. As founder and former CEO of Southwest Airlines, Herb Kelleher, has said: "If employees are treated right, they treat the outside world right, the outside world uses the company's product again, and that makes the shareholders happy." While having fun and embracing the zany might be less important to your older employees, it's paramount for your young professionals—many of whom are used to enjoying a yearly parade of celebrations at their secondary schools and colleges, including dances, carnivals, and parades.

BRING YOUR COMPANY'S HISTORY OFF THE WEB AND INTO YOUR WORK

One of the best reasons for a young professional to care about her company is if she understands how it got to where it is today. When I learned that the founder of a nonprofit I used to work for began the organization as a project for her graduate degree—and upon graduation turned down a string of high-paying nonprofit administration jobs to grow the small volunteer program into one of the largest arts education organizations in the country—you better believe I felt honored to be a member of her company and worked hard to earn her respect. Although sharing your company's history may be a formal part of your new hire orientation, which unfortunately means much of it will go in one ear and out the other due to nerves and information overload, I like to encourage managers to use stories and anecdotes of a company, its staff, and its customers on an ongoing basis to share institutional knowledge in a meaningful, memorable, and actionable way. A company's history needs to live in the collective consciousness and imagination of its employees, not simply in reports to clients, funders, or other stakeholders.

Hook young professionals with stories of current and preceding employees—particularly young ones—who have gone above and beyond their job descriptions. Explain specifically what they did that was noteworthy and what can be learned through their example. Just as importantly, let young professionals learn from employees who encountered obstacles and figured out how to overcome them. Perhaps your company laid off three-fourths of its employees to survive the economic downturn and is bringing on new staff for the first time in three years. Detail what senior leadership, management, and—if appropriate—you have learned through your company's lean years. On the flip side, if your company used to have a team of five and now has several thousand employees working throughout the world, deconstruct and evaluate how such growth transpired.

A nurse in one of my leadership groups at the Southern Nevada Medical Industry Coalition (SNMIC) once shared that her supervisor told her on her first day that another new nurse had recently challenged a doctor's diagnosis and that it saved a patient's life. While a lot of this nurse's peers felt that the supervisor was out of line and could be encouraging young nurses to challenge authority, the nurse telling the story swears it was the best part of her onboarding experience. "I felt so empowered" learning this piece of recent history, she explained. She felt for the first time like she had the permission to be a true patient advocate. "We're always told in school that our number one responsibility is to the patient. And yet the moment you get thrown onto a hospital floor you can easily be made to feel that you report to doctors. Knowing that a young nurse trusted her gut so much that when she saw something different than what a doctor did she spoke up has helped me trust my intuition so much more. I'm definitely a better nurse because of it."

DEMYSTIFY COMPANY AND FIELD JARGON

DAY 21

In addition to carrying their company's history in their bones, young professionals feel integrated into a company when they understand and can comfortably speak the language of their workplace tribe. While I once made a pact with myself that I wasn't going to use workplace learning and coaching jargon like "possibilities," "authenticity," or "integrity" for at least a week—and my blog post chronicling it was one of Brazen Careerist's Top Blog Posts of 2009 so it's safe to say the idea of dropping overused jargon resonated—having a command for a company's vernacular is important for young professionals to consider themselves participants rather than observers in your company. As soon as your young professionals can sink their teeth into their role—usually just before the end of month one—make sure that they also have been clued into the words, acronyms, and phrases that circulate your company and your industry—the useful, the clever, and the trite. Take comfort that explaining company lingo does not mean you have to encourage its usage. If you are in corporate social responsibility (CSR), for example—an important field that is comprised of jargon down to its very name—the way you feel about "triple bottom line" and "lasting impact" may very well resemble the way I feel about reality TV. Nonetheless, as someone who does a lot of work at the intersections of young professionals and pop culture, I need to be somewhat familiar with Kim Kardashian and Bethenny Frankel just like your young professionals need to be familiar with your own industry phrases.

MATCH YOUNG PROFESSIONALS WITH A PEER BUDDY

As we discussed in chapter 2, it is vital that young professionals have a great lunch experience on their first day—which usually means grabbing a bite and getting their gab on with one or more of their professional peers. When asked about her favorite parts of her company's onboarding culture, Sarah Miller, a young professional at Nourish International, pointed to having lunch with her peers on her first day as important as Nourish's monthly employee socials—which, should you want to steal a couple of good ideas, have included working collaboratively in a community garden and impromptu neighborhood ice cream dates. When young professionals feel bonded to their peers, they have people to turn to when they need to troubleshoot professional and personal obstacles, when they need to feel that desired sense of connection to a workplace community, and they usually stick around with their employer because they feel at home.

I recommend connecting young professionals with a specific peer buddy, ideally outside of the immediate team. This supports staff to develop a strong relationship within the workplace and gives them license to ask questions they might not feel comfortable asking their direct supervisor. It also gives them access to a different perspective than those they encounter daily. Having a confidant a few degrees removed from the team gives a young professional the opportunity to troubleshoot obstacles that emerge with somebody who most likely does not have a stake in the outcome. Yet because she is a part of the company's culture and most likely knows the key players involved in the situation, she can offer advice that somebody completely removed from the workplace cannot.

SET UP MEET AND GREETS WITH KEY CONTACTS

DAY 14

At the end of the last chapter you learned the importance of providing contact information to young professionals for the people they will need to work with on an ongoing basis. While as a generation your young professionals are masters of building relationships online, their ability to pick up the phone to schedule a face-to-face meeting leaves much to be desired. We will address how to develop young professionals' communication competencies in the next chapter. In the meantime, if you want your new hires to feel comfortable doing the work you have hired them to do as quickly as possible, take it one step further than giving them contact info. If you see, as I anticipate you will, that they have no problem sending a text or messaging a contact on Twitter, yet pace around their office anytime they need to pick up the phone and set up an appointment, throw them a bone by setting up face-to-face meetings with the people they are going to be interfacing with—particularly those outside your office walls.

Keep introductory meetings informal and introduce young professionals in a way that sets them up to feel equal parts confident and independent. For example, imagine that you have brought your young professional to a meeting with Gabrielle, a director at Gnarly Notebooks. *Gabrielle, I'd like to introduce you to Sean—our newest account exec. I'm going to be transitioning day-to-day oversight of your account to him over the next month. If you're half as blown away as I've been by his ability to get Gnarly Notebooks exactly what they want out of our creative department, you can thank me with a gift certificate for two at a steakhouse.* As you notice young professionals finding their footing in their new relationships, step back from driving the conversation and let them take over—if possible, even during the first meeting you set up. *I've got a conference call I've got to scoot back to the office for. Thank you both for taking the time to get together with me. Gabrielle, we'll talk soon. Sean, see you back at the office this afternoon.* The goal is to get in, help young professionals get comfortable, and then get out. Ensuring that your young professionals get off on the right foot with the people whose relationships will determine their—and most likely, if you are a supervisor, your success—does require an upfront investment of time and energy. As I believe you will see upon implementation, however, when young professionals are given the resources (interpersonal as well as material) to feel comfortable and work autonomously, you give yourself far more time and energy on the backend.

DAY 14 — BE TRANSPARENT ABOUT AFTER-HOURS

You've accepted the fact that as someone charged with the success of young professional new hires you have to do a bit of professional matchmaking. You ensure that a new employee has a lunch date on day one and a peer buddy to turn to for support during the onboarding process. Now, it's time to be clear about what is and isn't appropriate between 5 p.m. and 9 a.m. and on weekends.

While some of these policies may be outlined in a fair amount of detail in your HR manual or discussed during orientation, don't assume that if you are a manager, you are off the hook here. Even if young professionals know they cannot date a direct supervisor or throw a party in your conference room on Saturday night, they may not draw the conclusion that they need to notify you if they are dating a fellow member of their team. Or that if they are planning to hold a meeting after-hours, they still need to clear it to ensure there's no double booking of space. Does your company support social drinking in the workplace? Are employees allowed or maybe even encouraged to socialize and build relationships with their supervisors and more senior leaders? Let young professionals know how to play nice and be appropriate with each other once they are off the clock.

Being transparent about after-hours also means letting young professionals know about opportunities they can take advantage of to develop a stronger connection to your culture. Perhaps your company has an informal biking group that rides together the first Sunday of each month. Or maybe there's an unwritten code that each time somebody gets promoted you all take her bowling the weekend after to celebrate. It's also beneficial to give young professionals a heads-up about what to expect at their first company birthday or holiday party. Is it common practice for people to give a small gift to each person in the department? Bring a dessert? Wear a crazy Santa outfit?

At one environmental consulting firm, the founder and president of the small company holds a big Christmas extravaganza each year. While employees are always notified that there is a buffet-style dinner, white elephant gift exchange, and even an awards ceremony to honor staff in such areas as "The Most Wildlife Encounters" to "The Best Dressed," there also is an unwritten practice where senior staff haze the newer staff by giving them an obscene number of free shots. One young employee got so violently ill after his first Christmas party that he thought he had alcohol poisoning. "A heads-up on the expectation to be a drinking machine would have meant that I showed up with a full stomach and had a transportation plan that did not involve me driving myself home," he says. If you want your young professionals to work smart, show them how to play smart...and with each other. As the most social generation in the workplace—on average building and maintaining 500–1000 relationships through face-to-face and online relationship building—young professionals are more likely to stick around and be contributing members of a community if they feel they are a valued member of it.

DAY 30 GIVE A ROLE AT MEETINGS

Your young professionals can be beastly in meetings. They text, tweet, talk to the person they're sitting next to, and twiddle their thumbs. In other words, they model the behavior they see around them. But because young professionals are oftentimes more performative with their disinterest and are the lowest gal or guy on the totem pole, it's the youngest generation's behavior bemoaned whenever I talk to a group about how to jazz up company meetings.

While I understand you may be feeling like your young professionals still should know better, I'd rather spend our time together and see you use your energy to reframe this behavioral obstacle into an opportunity for additional employee engagement.

Recall for a moment manager Chris from chapter 2. As part of the first day experience for Chris's young professional, Chris has the employee design the PowerPoint template that will be used in the meeting—which Chris publicly acknowledges the employee for—and asks the new hire to record top takeaways. While this is a hypothetical example, the simple practices of asking a young professional to do something in advance for a meeting, honoring good work in front of colleagues, and having a young professional play a role in a meeting creates the opportunity for engagement to occur.

If this sounds like a lot to do each time you have one of your young professionals attend a meeting, rest assured you don't have to employ each strategy each time. While you cover appropriate behavior during company meetings with your young professional when you cover your other workplace expectations, you make it easy for them to stay off their gadgets at meetings by giving them a reason to be present in mind as well as body. And the more the role you give your young professionals involves some form of presentation—even if it's simply to share a couple of your ideas afterward—the more you will help them flex their communication abilities and develop confidence and the ability to speak for maximum impact.

ADMIT WHEN YOU HAVE EGG ON YOUR FACE

DAY 30

While young professionals are often chastised by their employers for failing to admit their mistakes—a learned behavior, perhaps?—they simply melt when their supervisors and companies take accountability for their own mishaps. Keep in mind that this is the first generation of employees who have known intimate details about the extramarital sex lives of their presidents and people in Congress. They have seen their parents forced to postpone retirement due to an economic crisis facilitated—at least in part—by corporate greed and unethical decision making. Blogs, reality shows, and tell-all memoirs—popular media for your young professionals—are predicated on their subjects revealing their messiest mistakes. For young professionals, however, breaches of trust rarely happen for making an error—no matter how egregious it might be. Young professionals distrust people and institutions when those in positions of power strive to sweep their mistakes under the rug and then pretend to ignore the big old carpet bulge in the middle of their offices.

Because accountability and operating from a place of integrity are qualities young professionals look for in their managers, leaders, and company as a whole, model responsible ownership of mistakes. Culture, above all else, is comprised of the behaviors of everyone in the workplace. So if you pass a policy that after implementation has proven nearsighted, call it out and adjust it. Be transparent about why the error happened, and how you will make sure it doesn't happen again. Similarly, if you realize that choices you are making are not in alignment with one or more of your organizational core values or your company vision or mission—perhaps you've been inflexible about employee schedule changes when one of your mantras is work hard, play hard—make the "oops" a teachable moment and show your young professionals that they are part of a culture where mistakes can happen. The irony is that when they recognize that they have permission to fail, your young professionals will respect you and your company enough to self-correct many of the common newbie mistakes—sending out emails without proofreading, or presenting financial statements where calculations haven't been triple checked—that are the least conducive to learning and growth.

By creating a culture where mistakes can happen, you also are urging your young professionals to push themselves slightly outside of their comfort zone—where the smartest, most innovative work takes place. As a generation used to being lauded for everything from taking out the trash to paying off charges they accrued on their *parents'* credit card, your young professionals are likely entering the workplace with a fair amount of risk aversion. If you want them to invest fully in their work at your company, you need to figure out how to provide feedback that honors their history of frequent praise. You also need to support them to risk failing, which really can only happen if they know you won't view a snafu as grounds for a pink slip or public shaming.

CO-CREATE A CULTURE OF GLOBAL RESPONSIBILITY

DAY 60

CSRWire.com, the leading source of information on corporate social responsibility and sustainable workplace practices reported in 2011:

- 83 percent of Generation Y trust a company if it is socially/environmentally responsible.

- 79 percent want to work for a company that cares about how it affects and contributes to society.

- 69 percent are aware of their employer's commitment to social and environmental causes.

- 64 percent say their company's social and environmental activities make them feel loyal to that company.

- And perhaps the most shocking, 56 percent would refuse to work for an irresponsible corporation.

If you are struggling to connect your young professionals to a compelling part of your company culture, use what your company is doing that is good for society and good for the environment as a hook. Ideally, this is not simply using Seventh Generation hand soap in your bathroom or placing recycling bins in the break room. Your young professionals want—and in my opinion, deserve—to see evidence of a long-term social and environmental sustainability vision. If your company does not have a fully realized CSR policy, has not established giving programs, or if you are looking for a way to grow a young professional's leadership skill set, offer her opportunities to shape your company's giving culture. Perhaps she can spearhead a project to bring potable water to a rural community in a developing nation or bring mentors from your company to your local prison to teach computer and interview skills necessary for re-entry. When you do good for society and empower your staff to be socially-conscious leaders, you have the added benefit of making your company attractive to and credible with other civic-minded young professionals—as fans, customers, and future employees.

Given young professionals' affinity for companies that do good work in and outside of their four walls, I was not surprised that as I collected stories for this book, I had the easiest time culling best onboarding practices from employees at socially and environmentally conscious companies. For example, Sarah Miller of Nourish International—who we heard from earlier in the chapter—says that one of her best experiences working for her social enterprise—a student movement to eradicate global poverty—was designing the company's global education curriculum. Initially Sarah's supervisor was excited to spearhead the creation of a series of educational modules for students on international development. But when she learned that Sarah had lived and taught in the developing world, she delegated the project to Sarah because she knew she was the right person to take the lead. Sarah says "I am very proud and happy to work with a team that takes aligning work with our strengths so seriously."

CONNECT BOOK KNOWLEDGE TO THE REALITIES OF THE WORKPLACE

Your college-educated young professionals most likely come to you with tremendous book knowledge. More importantly, they are masters at the "one-minute research project"—meaning you ask them a question and they rather magically enter the right search terms to give a deceptively complete answer based on less than a minute or two of online research. Yet even if your young professionals can wow you with the history, global impact, and a comparative analysis of companies offering your clients' products or services, if they are charged with marketing your products or services, they still need experience creating a campaign before they can be called effective in their role. It's important to show your young professionals that it's not enough to present themselves as fits in the culture of the work or to be able to give the right answers. They need a keen understanding of how to produce the specific results you are measuring their success upon, and this understanding can only come from young professionals actually producing them.

There are two effective ways to give your young professionals the opportunity to transfer book knowledge into real-world knowledge. One, give it to them. And I'm not trying to be funny or snarky here. You can talk to young professionals until there's smoke coming out of their ears about "how" to do something. But remember, this is the 30-second sound-byte generation. They won't let you deposit information into them for very long before they divert their attention to something they find more engaging— even if it's simply daydreaming of sunning in St. Maarten. Get them actually doing their work as quickly as possible. Through their performance and the way you facilitate their reflection upon it—more on this in the coming example and in chapter 6—they will learn.

Second, for tasks and projects where there just isn't a lot of room for learning errors (for example, nurses, lawyers, and teachers don't have the luxury to learn on the job without some serious consequences), you can use role play to simulate the conditions and culture of the work. During periods of time where your young professionals do not have to be "on," give them the opportunity to step into increasingly responsible roles, develop the thinking and behavior that is critical for their success, and provide opportunities to help them solidify what is working and recognize and reshape what is not.

When constructing a role play, be very specific about the scenario and what you are asking young professionals to do in it prior to starting. Explain what they need to know about the people they will be playing and what roles you or anyone else in the role play will be embodying. Without stepping into characters, role play doesn't work effectively. It either devolves into more hypothetical discussion, or the people involved feel like they are playing themselves. The latter limits risk taking and can make a young professional feel exposed. Finally, give a brief overview about how you will be facilitating the role-play experience. Will you simply be timing for 10 minutes and letting whatever happens, happen, because you will be debriefing what transpired later? Or as the facilitator will you yell "stop" at various points, everyone will momentarily step out of role, and then you will introduce new pieces of the role play? Make sure everyone knows the rules of the game before asking them to play it.

It's one thing to talk about motivating apathetic middle school students. As we will explore together in the role play, it's an entirely different thing to put a young professional into a hypothetical middle school classroom culture with unruly, angsty, and insecure middle school students and tell her to hook them with Shakespeare. This role play is one that I have led through the Creative Arts Team at The City University of New York for middle school teachers who want to develop coaching strategies to engage their students in exploring Shakespeare's language and themes. A hypothetical middle school English department chair—who we will call Ed—has invited new English teachers in his department for a professional development training. His intention is to give his new teachers easy-to-apply, interactive strategies to help them hook their fifth through eighth grade students in their exploration of Shakespeare's plays. As you read through the role play, observe how Ed sets up the learning culture, runs, and then debriefs what he has done, so that his young professionals are able to transfer what they have learned into action.

Teacher Terrance Motivates Middle School Students

Ed: To support everyone in their Shakespeare units, I want to give you a way to show your students that whatever they are interested in can be found in Shakespeare before you ever hand them a script. For the next five minutes or so, I'm asking you to pretend that my name is Terrance and I'm your sixth grade English teacher. I give you full permission to sit in your seats and participate as your students would as I lead you in a mock English lesson. You can have fun being sassy and challenging me as you think they would, but at the same time I want you to keep your teacher hat on. The end goal is that you are able to take what I have done and lead the work in your classroom, so it's important that as you play along, you are also seeing how I am moving from one thing to the next. Any questions before we get started?

Holly: Just one, Ed. To clarify, the answers I give should not reflect what I know and rather what I think my students know or would say?

Ed: Exactly.

Holly: Awesome. This is going to be a blast. (Holly slumps down into her seat, crosses her arms across her chest, and lets out an exasperated sigh.)

Ed: Well done, Holly. So if there aren't any other questions, I'm going to ask you to adopt a particular middle school persona, even select a new name for yourself, and we'll get started. We're going to stay in our roles until I announce that the role play is over. And...we're entering the role play. 3-2-1 Action. (Ed adjusts his posture and puts on a sport jacket). Good morning, everyone. I'm really excited for the unit we're about to begin. We're going to be taking a look at a classic story that you could find today on TV or in the movies. And although our story happened hundreds of years ago, I think it's one you're going to really like.

Murphy: I doubt that, Mr. T.

Ed: Ah, a challenge from...

Murphy: Eduardo.

Ed: Yes, Eduardo, tell me...if you were going to make a movie or TV show about anything you wanted...what would it be about?

Murphy: Violence. Lots of people killing each other. So see, not going to happen, is it?

Jennie: I would want mean girls in it, Mr. Terrance. Or at least one mean girl. Someone everyone is scared of yet they totally worship her.

Ed: Okay, I'm writing on the board violence, murder, and a mean girl. What else would make a story interesting for you?

Paul: How about some totally crazy people. Maybe they're psychics. Or homeless. Or both.

Ed: Why is this important to you?

Paul: I like the idea of outcasts being the people who actually know what's going on.

(Imagine that this goes on for a while and that Teacher Terrance continues to make each of his students right. He asks for clarification as necessary to forward learning).

Ed: Now we've got A LOT of different ideas up here. (He reads each one back.) And you know, most of them are in the story we're going to be reading. It's about a guy named Macbeth. (He explains the basic plot and shows how most of the brainstormed ideas apply.) Now, everyone, I'm taking off Teacher Terrance, and I'd like each of you to let go of your middle school identities, as compelling as they were. And let's deconstruct this working backward from where we are now back to the beginning to see how it happened. So let me ask you, where are we?

Murphy: You pretty seamlessly just showed us how everything we would want to make a movie or TV show about is in the play we're going to be studying.

Ed: Great.

Murphy: And it's super cool that you never said the word "play," which is something most of my students have never heard of. You called it a story. And said it was something they could see in TV or in the movies.

Ed: I'm glad you noticed this, Murphy. While I would certainly explain a play as a precursor to movies and TV shows in a future lesson, to do that before getting them excited about the story is just going to disengage them. So what happened just before I revealed the basic premise of Macbeth?

Jennie: You read all of our ideas. This helped us see that we each had a voice and that you took what we said seriously enough to write it on the board.

Ed: And how about the initial brainstorm? What did you notice about how I set it up and how I kept it going?

Paul: You said that you liked what we were going to be doing, and then you asked for our ideas in a way that felt like we were going to get to study what we wanted to study. That was really cool.

Holly: I'm wondering though, Ed, what happens if someone says something that's totally inappropriate or that doesn't exist in the play we're doing?

Ed: This is a great question, Holly. When someone says something off the wall, I choose to still write it down to diffuse it. Because if our students are thinking about it, pretending we didn't hear it or shutting it down either makes them feel invisible or in too many cases just gives them attention for being thorns in our side. And then the conversation goes underground where we can't make it teachable. So if somebody says "sex," I might push back and say, "Okay, so you'd like to see romantic relationships." Or I might ask, "What shows have you seen that do an interesting job showing the love lives of its characters?" If what they say doesn't fit into the world of the play, I'll still put it up there because it may be that what they like is a great image or metaphor in the world of the play. With *Twilight* and *True Blood* being so popular, you might get a student saying "vampires." A vampire can be a person who sucks your energy. So if we were looking at *Romeo and Juliet* in my class, I could ask, "Who are the 'vampires' for Juliet?"

Holly: Thanks, that really helps.

Ed: Let me keep being helpful to you. What do you need to know to be able to lead the lesson that I modeled today? (Ed then goes on to answer any lingering questions and helps the teachers customize their lead-in for introducing their specific play.)

In order for your young professionals to execute tasks as successfully as they regurgitate information on tests, you want to construct a culture for them to transfer their knowledge into action as easily and as quickly as possible. As soon as the role play ended, Ed asked questions to ensure his young teachers understood how to take what he had led and facilitate the curriculum with their students. By asking the participants to replay what he did, step-by-step, he enabled them to ingrain their learning. Ed gave the English teachers opportunities to ask questions so that he could help them identify adaptations they could make to best meet their students' needs and desires. And throughout the role play and the processing of it, Ed balanced creating a fun learning environment with replicating the actual environment that the teachers would be entering into to make the role play a true rehearsal space for future action.

Hitch your young professionals to your company culture—from the way you let them feel when they walk in the door each morning, to how you allow them to learn and produce results, to what they have to look forward to in and outside of work hours. If and when possible, get your young professionals involved not only in contributing to but also in sharing their experiences with your company both to animate recruitment and to keep them invested. Give them the chance to connect what they have learned to what they have to do and create opportunities to rehearse the skills and behaviors they are expected to employ. And because the key component of a company's culture is its people, most importantly, make new employee relationship building a central part of your onboarding culture.

For example, at Realty Executive of Nevada, owner/broker Fafie Moore has developed an entire young professionals group to build community among her young real estate agents. The group is currently spearheaded by Lauren Barbarich, a young professional, and provides a space for young agents—both those young in age and those young to the profession—to come together to have fun. Whether schmoozing at a new bar, watching a concert, or going to a casino pool, it gives employees the opportunity to build relationships and feel a deeper sense of connection to their company. And according to Lauren, while the aim for the time being is primarily social, she can already see the impact on performance. "When we feel comfortable with the people we work with, we're much more likely to ask questions and get the support we need before and when problems emerge. We serve our clients better and have the resources to close more transactions. In many ways, our group is the training ground for future leadership in the profession."

Tweet-Sized Takeaways

- **Give young professionals workplace rituals and traditions that get them jazzed.**
- **Share inspiring stories about your company's history on an ongoing basis.**
- **Explain industry terms to young professionals so they feel included in your tribe.**
- **Connect young professionals with a peer buddy.**
- **Arrange easy breezy meetings for your new hires with their key contacts.**
- **Help young professionals be appropriately social and engaged with their colleagues outside of work.**
- **If you want them to be present in mind as well as body at company meetings, give them compelling reasons to be.**

- **Remember that young professionals respect people and companies that make their mistakes learning opportunities.**

- **Engage young professionals in co-creating programs and policies that make positive social and environmental impact.**

- **Foster a rich learning and development culture that creates a bridge between book and required real-world knowledge.**

93

chapter 5:

Build High-Impact Communicators

"Good communication is as stimulating as black coffee and just as hard to sleep after."

Anne Morrow Lindbergh

One of the most common deficits young professionals enter the workplace with is a lack of professional communication skills. And unfortunately, for young professionals and you, this deficit in communication is actually a combination of many deficits that run the gamut from a lack of professionalism, to not choosing the right medium for one's audience, to a general inability to construct a well-developed, coherent argument. The reasons for these consistent communication blunders are numerous. First, there has been an increase in academic standardized testing, reducing the amount of educational time spent engaged in hands-on learning. Second, young professionals as we know spend a lot of time online and in front of a screen. And third, to be perfectly honest, the generation has placed little value on the skill or time developing professional communication skills.

You would be hard-pressed to find a study identifying anything other than communication as the number one skill employers look for in a prospective new hire. And public speaking is consistently ranked as the number one fear for people throughout the world. Yet most young professionals, unless they are communication majors, have taken just one or two communication courses in college. For me, and hopefully you, this is troubling.

Although college is supposed to prepare young people to be confident and competitive in the workforce—and to recap, employers really want good communicators, and people irrespective of age are terrified of public speaking—college students are not required and usually don't select to take more than three to six credit hours to develop the competency. It's easy to blame college communication programs for not hooking students into taking more courses, or for not doing enough during their one to two touches with the average college students. And given that I taught college public speaking for a number of years, I'm familiar with how most college students think about their introductory communication courses! But more importantly, I'm also aware of how just a little focused, smart work can meet young people where they are in their communication and get them where they need to be. In addition to having my college students perform their required informative and persuasive speeches, I made sure that they also learned how to successfully give a professional introduction, answer common interview questions, run an informational interview, and provide action-oriented feedback to their peers. Most of my students got

As and Bs despite my being a rigorous grader. And my communication students still write me about how they are procuring jobs from informational interviews!

While every company necessitates a different kind of communicator, from my experience and research prepping young professionals to be dynamic speakers, I've identified a few core competencies that transcend a particular company, culture, or community. In this chapter, you will learn how to help young professionals recognize their own communication styles, and the styles of their supervisors and team members. You will explore how to assist young professionals in flexing their styles to meet the needs of the audience. You will learn a simple technique for effortlessly organizing thoughts into easy-to-follow, well-substantiated proposals. Finally, you will discover how to teach your new hires how to carry an audience with them from one idea to the next, speak with confidence and clarity, and give themselves permission *not* to be perfect so that they can make progress.

EXCHANGE COMMUNICATION PREFERENCES AND STYLES

DAY 7

Young professional career and workplace expert, Lindsey Pollak, created a wonderful exercise in her opinion piece, "The Best Way to Communicate in the Workplace" for *ABCNews on Campus* that I use with young professionals all the time. Lindsey gives the following scenario.

Kylie is stuck in traffic, running late for a meeting with her supervisor, Danielle. Danielle is a pretty mellow boss, only a few years older than Kylie, but she is strict about the importance of being on time. Should Kylie:

A) Call Danielle's office phone.

B) Call Danielle's cell phone.

C) Text Danielle.

D) Send Danielle an email from her iPhone.

In case you're wondering, most college students and young professionals are divided between B and D. But as Lindsey points out, there is no "right" conclusion you can draw from the information you have. All of the answers *could* be "right." What Kylie needs to ask to discover the right answer for her and Danielle is, "How would Danielle want me to communicate that I'm running late?"

It's easy to draw sweeping generalizations about what is "appropriate" communication. And in the next tactic, I'll go ahead and show you which ones are safe to teach young professionals to draw. But for most people, it's not about always talking, texting, or tweeting. It's about having a preference for a particular medium in a particular situation. Engage young professionals in a conversation about the different contexts your team communicates in and what each person's preferences are in your department. Five of the most important areas to cover include:

- delivering to-do lists and reminders

- sharing large quantities of information

- communicating last minute or time sensitive information

- after-hours communication

- brainstorming or idea generation.

Now, if you're going to ask your young professionals to be audience-centered and communicate via the medium that the person they are communicating with most wants, you need to be willing to similarly shake up your delivery mode. If your young professional has expressed that for after-hours, or for communicating time sensitive information, she prefers a Facebook message to a work email, then *please* use Facebook. Ever wonder why those who teach middle or high school say "ignant" (meaning, ignorant) or "s'up" (meaning, what's up) as much as their students? It's not a last ditch effort to hold onto their youth or a sign that educators are ill-equipped to perform their important work. Developing communication muscles is as much about internalizing what we see and hear as what we do and make habit. So if you want young employees to flex to meet you where you are, make sure you model the importance of this practice by flexing to meet them where they are.

In addition to knowing how the people they work closely with prefer to communicate contextually, it's useful for young professionals to be able to identify their guiding communication style and the main style of their co-workers. Preference and style are often used interchangeably to great detriment.

Preference Vs. Style

A **preference** is one's choice about how to perform a particular task or project. When discussing communication, a preference shifts according to a situation and is directly linked to the medium one is selecting. **Style**, on the other hand, is one's natural way of thinking and doing. It is not project, task, or situation specific. Style stays relatively consistent over time and across context. It reflects a person's most comfortable and efficient way of working.

I currently subscribe to the prevailing belief that there are four basic communication styles: **doers** and **thinkers** (who are task-based) and **influencers** and **connectors** (who are relationship-based). Most people, with just a minimal amount of description, can identify their core communication style. Doers like communication that leads to immediate action. They are results-driven, enjoy being in control and possessing power, and typically couldn't care less about the details. Thinkers are information gatherers. They are slow and methodical in communication and decision making. They enjoy a lot of structure and although they can be shy, they also relish a sense of winning or being right. Influencers like to think out loud to formulate their ideas. They are typically creative and fun people to be around. Although they thrive on human interaction, they are known to cut people off in conversation because they so quickly jump from one thought to the next. Connectors like to know their exact responsibilities and work with others, as long as there is adequate time for trust to be built. Connectors tend not to take big risks and feel most comfortable engaged in getting work completed. Acknowledgement, as long as it's given privately, means the world to them.

Don't get caught up in which theory or assessment tool you use when having conversations with your young professionals about communication. If the four types I shared work for you, great. If not, find a way of talking about or assessing a communication style that does. Focus on what each person's style looks and feels like in practice and how you and the members of your team can set each other up for success.

 ## KEEP COMMUNICATION AUDIENCE-APPROPRIATE

Knowing one's communication preferences and style helps a person communicate from a place of power. Knowing the way colleagues like to communicate enables you to sculpt your message so that they can best hear and take appropriate action from it. Knowing what's appropriate for a particular audience is a different, equally important muscle you want your young professionals to flex so that the moment-to-moment communication choices they make reflect well on them, you, and your company.

A typical young professional is likely to communicate with the following key audiences—supervisor or manager, department or cross-departmental peer, upper management or senior leadership, recurring customers or clients, prospective customers or clients, former customers or clients, and business or community stakeholders. When young professionals first have interactions with people in these various categories, they are unlikely to know their communication preferences or style. The more you make this a part of your onboarding, though, the more adept they'll be at picking up cues from other people they come into contact with. Support them to make the right choices about medium to use, tone to adopt, level of preparation, and level of proofreading that is necessary for communication to land with a bang with each particular audience.

By detailing your expectations for communication with each of the groups your young professionals come into contact with, you also ensure that time is being allocated appropriately. While on the surface it may sound like a good policy to browbeat grammatical errors out of all correspondence, if you or I spend as much time on a text message we sent to our significant other as we spend on a report going to a potential funder, we wouldn't be very efficient. So while I don't care if an email I receive from my assistant has a typo, smiley face, or shorthand, she knows I'll have her head—or at least her ear—if anything goes out on my behalf that hasn't been quadruple checked for grammar, content, and tone.

ILLUMINATE GENERATIONAL PREFERENCES

DAY 45

While not as time sensitive as the first two tactics, you also want to demystify generational preferences. Again, I want to reiterate that by shining a light on generational differences, I'm not giving you license to traffic in generalizations. Nor do I want to ingrain stereotypes. I do, however, want to illuminate the researched and proven differences between how the generations transfer, absorb, and think about communication. For the first time in our nation's history, we have four generations in the workplace, and each has a very different approach and appreciation for communication. While there are no universally agreed upon dates for each generation, to make sure we're on the same page, I use the following—**Traditionalists** or the **Silent Generation** (born between the mid-1920s and mid-1940s), **Baby Boomers** (born between the mid-1940s and mid-1960s), **Generation X** (born between the mid-1960s and late-1970s) and finally your young professionals, **Generation Y** or **Millennials** (born between the late 1970s and 2000).

Many of your organization's senior leaders are Traditionalists. As a 30-million person generation that came of age during World War II, Traditionalists are incredibly patriotic, have a tremendous respect for authority, and are incredibly rule-bound. When they communicate, Traditionalists like to see the research to back up an opinion. They want to know how experts are weighing in. They like to have policies in place to ensure work is systematized and operating "by-the-book." Traditionalists often don't create space for everybody to have voice in a conversation, and instead they prefer for work to happen in committees with a designated leader to facilitate, report back, and be accountable. While most generations are comfortable moving between communication mediums, for Traditionalists, face-to-face communication is preferred, followed shortly after by the phone, and only then followed by email and social media.

Baby Boomers make up about 30 percent of the workplace—although this percentage will continue to shrink until your young professionals overtake them around 2016—and are incredibly work-centric, achievement-oriented, and competitive. With approximately 75 million of them, their values have shaped what constitutes "normal" workplace cultural attitudes—"Work hard and you will succeed." "Everyone has to pay their dues." "There's no shortcut to success." Traditionalists work hard because it's the right thing to do; Baby Boomers work hard because they believe it is the key to success. Baby Boomers like to speak about vision and are masters of messages that inspire people to dream bigger. Oprah Winfrey is perhaps the best example of this. Because they are adrenaline junkies, they respond to change pretty well and are incredibly excited by brainstorming and new possibilities. When Baby Boomers communicate, they place as much stock in body language as in the words being used to communicate. They expect the people they are communicating with to have devised multiple possibilities and be flexible in their thinking.

Generation X is often referred to as the lost generation. Small in number—just above 45 million—Generation X has not received nearly as much attention from demographers as Baby Boomers or Generation Y/Millennials. They are a generation for whom 50 percent of their parents' marriages ended in divorce. As a result, many were raised in single-parent households where they learned to be self-reliant. X'ers have been stereotyped in 1990s coming of age movies like *Wayne's World, Dazed and Confused,* and *Reality Bites* as distrusting authority and possessing a "whatever" attitude. While members of this generation may not show their drive like the generations surrounding them—working 70-hour weeks or asking how to get promoted on their first day at work, respectively— Generation X should be noted for being the most technologically advanced generation and for their focus on questioning authority in pursuit of doing work that achieves results. Members of Generation X tend to be independent, deep thinkers and don't have a great love for team-oriented cultures. They like to bring in technology whenever possible, and they do it at a higher-level than your young professionals. While Millennials might be on Facebook as much as they can get away with—primarily to socialize—Generation X uses technology such as webinars, video conferencing, and live video streaming to share information and give and receive feedback efficiently, often in real time.

While Generation X was the first generation of latchkey children, Generation Y youth often came home from school each day to a fresh plate of cookies, classical music, scented candles, and a note from mom professing her love. We've already unpicked stereotypes for the generation, and I encourage you to let your young professionals tell you what they believe is true about them and their peers. Do they believe as a generation that they truly work best in teams, thrive in a culture of diversity, and value making a positive impact over bringing home a six-figure paycheck? And most importantly, do they agree that they best process information in short, easy-to-digest sound bites? Is it true that they find themselves most engaged when people speak to them conversationally and make them a part of finding a solution? Do they express their feelings more openly than their older professional peers?

Let discussions about generational communication preferences be ongoing, like most of the other onboarding tactics. If a young professional is about to meet with a new client who is a Traditionalist, speak with her about how she will present her information so the client can best absorb it. Rather than a five-minute conversational presentation with PowerPoint, perhaps the young professional will lead in with two successful case studies and sprinkle statistics and findings from industry whitepapers throughout. If your department is intergenerational—as more and more are—strategize about how you can communicate in a way that respects preferences, style, and generational inclinations so that everyone is engaged.

MAKE OPINIONS SUB VS. MAIN ARGUMENTS

DAY 14

Whether communicating to a Traditionalist or a member of her own generation, effective young professional communicators do not build their arguments upon "I feel" or "I think" statements. When you share this with your young professionals they may very well agree with you, but know that their understanding does not necessarily translate into them easily performing the communication behaviors you seek. As you undoubtedly have witnessed, your young professionals have a habit of speaking as if they are in a therapy session. "I feel like what our department needs is more opportunities to work from home." "I think painting the office would boost employee morale." Oftentimes their thoughts and feelings will be spot on. Yet, it doesn't make for the most compelling argument.

Young professionals also may be lazy when acting on your message that they need backup for their arguments. In the age of instant access to information and so-called expert opinions, all it takes is 30 seconds and an Internet connection to find *somebody* with a flashy title to support a claim. When I was teaching speech classes, it amused me when two students would be taking opposite sides of a topic such as the death penalty. The first would say something like, "The death penalty is a necessary means to punish those who have taken life and is far less expensive than jailing people until they die." Then, the next one would lead in exactly the opposite way. "The death penalty needs to be abolished because it's costing citizens millions of dollars every year." My students did not understand that both arguments were partly right and wrong. They needed support, just like many of your young professionals undoubtedly will, to unpick the source of the issue—in this case that administering the death penalty itself is of course cheaper than paying for a lifetime in prison, but the litigation and appeals process for someone sentenced to death is what costs the United States millions of dollars each year.

So as you support young professionals to use evidence to substantiate a claim, help them to cull the right evidence: facts, testimony, and examples that not only are accurate, unbiased, and speak to the particular situation that they are addressing, but that can also be backed up by other equally unbiased facts, testimony, examples, and so forth. To return to the example of working from home, it's much more compelling to say, "Employees who telecommute enjoy a 10–15 percent productivity increase according to a recent survey of the American Telecommuting Association (ATA). And based on what I've tracked within our four walls, our numbers may be even higher. When people in our department have been able to complete their quarterly reports at home, we have an average turnaround time of 48 hours. When we do them in the office, our turnaround time is 72–96 hours. Therefore, I'm proposing that we make it standard policy that everyone in the department, irrespective of role, has two to four work-from-home writing days per quarter."

IDENTIFY THE CALL TO ACTION AND WORK BACKWARD

DAY 14

To support young professionals in how to organize their thinking, make a habit of first identifying what you want a person receiving a message to take away. Yes, I know, this notion of a **call to action** sounds like it's been plucked straight out of

Communication 101. And it has been. For when your young professionals know what they want to drive home, they can then easily take a step back and identify what they need to cover beforehand. From their call to action, they can decide how to structure a **conclusion**—both to summarize their main points and to leave listeners with something to consider moving forward. Next, they can take another step back and identify a few main points that create the **body** of their argument. Finally, they can take one final step back to their **introduction**. Knowing how they will sequentially move through their argument, they can think of a logical and inviting way to capture their audience's attention, establish their credibility, and introduce where they are headed.

This process works as well for presentations as it does for everyday professional workplace conversations. Most young professionals are more familiar—and therefore more comfortable—with impromptu, stream of consciousness social media messaging than substantive face-to-face discourse. Giving them a simple way to organize their thinking by working backward from their call to action to their introduction sets them up to be more impactful in their communication and ultimately more focused on the results they are striving to achieve. Let's look briefly at this in practice.

Amos Makes the Case for Wilshire Water

Amos is a young professional new hire at the Wilshire Water Company. He is about to have a follow-up conversation on the phone with a small business owner, Lorraine, who is contemplating leaving Wilshire and its water cooler service. She is being lured to a Wilshire competitor offering a discount. Amos has received some top-notch onboarding from his manager so he knows that he needs to go into the call with a loose script that works backward from his call to action to his introduction to make his case. Let's see how Amos sculpts it.

Call to Action: Are you ready to move forward with Wilshire?

(Note: In order for Amos to make this ask, he needs to have a bang-up conclusion that summarizes his main points and helps Lorraine not to make the decision based on price and rather on benefit.)

Conclusion: It sounds like your experiences with Wilshire have been just as terrific as mine. While you can't put a price on the health benefits you've noticed in yourself and your employees, or the customer service you've received over the phone and at your office, isn't an extra $25/month worth it to sustain what's been working so well for all of you?

(Note: Amos knows that Lorraine has always given Wilshire great reviews, so he has a good idea what her feedback will be during the call. In his main points, he wants to drive home the health benefits from ionized alkaline water—which only Wilshire provides—as well as the great customer service. He believes that by linking his positive experiences to Lorraine's he can best demonstrate this.)

Body:

Main point 1 (health benefits): I came to Wilshire Water after three years as a super satisfied customer. Since drinking Wilshire's ionized alkaline water, which as you may know is not offered by anyone else in the state, my embarrassing acne and skin discoloration completely cleared up. I noticed myself having more energy. I even got through three flu seasons without so much as a sniffle.

Main point 2 (customer service): One of my favorite parts about Wilshire is our service. We have someone at our local call center 14 hours a day. We respond to any problems with your device or changes in service within 24 hours, even over the weekend. That came in handy when I recently had family visiting and realized on a Friday night that I needed an extra bottle the next morning. Speaking of extra bottles, it's great that each person I share Wilshire with who calls our company gets a free five-gallon bottle for themselves and for me. I don't know any other vendor doing that as a thank you to its loyal customers.

Main point 3 (Lorraine's experiences): I'm most curious to learn about your experiences, Lorraine. I see that you've given us very good to excellent ratings on each of the three customer surveys you've filled out. Would you be willing to tell me about the impact Wilshire's water has had on your company's health? (Wait for an answer.) How about our customer service? What has most exceeded your expectations? (Wait for an answer.)

(Note: In his introduction, Amos wants to quickly capture Lorraine's attention, introduce the idea that he is not just a Wilshire rep but also a loyal customer, and outline where the conversation will go.)

Introduction: Thanks for giving me an opportunity to share why I came to work at Wilshire, Lorraine. I hope that my enthusiasm for our product coupled with your experiences with it will demonstrate why we're the company you want to drink with.

Now, when Amos makes his call he can start with his introduction, confident that he will be facilitating the conversation in such a way that he logically moves Lorraine to say "yes" by the time that he gets to his call to action.

WEED OUT VOCALIZED THINKING

Have you ever felt like a character straight out of *Gossip Girl* when you talk with one of your young professionals? "OMG, Selena. He like totally did not just, you know, do that thing he like is always doing, um, did he?" While "so, you know, like, um" and all those pesky little filler words are certainly not endemic to young professional speech. The more uncomfortable we are as face-to-face communicators, the more likely they are going to pop up. When we are nervous or when our heads move faster than our mouths, those words can't help but come out. And of course when they do, one sounds young and unprofessional.

The first thing you can do to support young professionals not to vocalize their thinking is to encourage them to slow down. Affectionately remind them that communication is not a race. Teach them to recognize when they are running out of breath, and interpret this as a sign to slow their rate of delivery. You can even play good cop by using a fun, mutually agreed upon hand gesture to draw attention to these speed-ups.

Second, help young professionals make a habit of bringing their sentences to a conclusion. As you've probably experienced, they often string two or three lengthy ideas together with an "and" or "but" or some other conjunction. Doing so makes it hard to follow their ideas and eliminates the natural time for breathing that happens at the end of a sentence. It also creates the opportunity for more of that awkward, vocalized thinking to emerge.

A final strategy to teach that is particularly useful if and when we lose our train of thought and ordinarily would drop an "and," "you know," "so," or "like" bomb is the stop-and-smile. It's as lovely and effortless as it sounds.

 As the name suggests, the **stop-and-smile** is when one feels a brain freeze coming on, she stops, smiles, (and breathes), finds her next idea, and then continues on.

I use it all the time when I'm presenting. And although I use it as a survival strategy not to break down, sweat, cry, or do all of the above when I forget where I'm headed, the irony is that it actually builds interest in and attention toward what is about to be spoken. Whether we're talking to an audience of one, 100, or 1000, they psychologically interpret the slow down in pacing as a sign that we're about to come out with something profound. We look our most confident when we take time to get our point across and dare to smile. It's a win-win for everyone.

 ## TAKE YOUR AUDIENCE WITH YOU

To continue the theme of best engaging an audience when we communicate, it's important for young professionals to learn to play nice with connectives—the cute and underutilized words and phrases that make it easy for someone to follow how they move between ideas and points. Let me be your time traveling guide back one more time to Communication 101. There are four types of connectives you want your young professionals to use.

 Transitions are brief statements that signal one is shifting gears between ideas. While they can be used anywhere in communication, they are particularly useful when moving from one part of a claim to the next: For example, from the introduction to the body or from a final main point to a conclusion. *Now that I've shared the three most important reasons to hire a director of onboarding, I'd like to explore who we could promote internally to fill this vital role.*

Internal previews and **internal summaries** perform just as their names suggest. They signal where a speaker is going within an idea or where she has just been. *Let's break down the three most important reasons to hire a director of onboarding* (internal preview). *To recap, the three most important reasons to hire a director of onboarding are to increase retention, reduce expenses associated with new hire errors, and lay the foundation for leadership development from day one* (internal summary).

Finally, **signposts** signal exactly where you are in your discussion. When I say "finally," you know this is my last point. If I say "first," you know I'm just beginning. Injecting other signposts like "next" and "after" efficiently help a listener know exactly where you are.

Signposts, just like transitions, internal previews, and internal summaries, empower young professionals to make their communication about others. Even though their heads might move faster than their mouths, when they are able to expose the seams of how they are thinking and how one of their ideas relates to the next, they will keep their audiences on their page.

CURB PEOPLE PLEASING AND PUFFING

In a culture that rewards the newest, flashiest, and often most unusual (and increasingly deviant and prurient behaviors) with fame and fortune, your young professionals who have grown up having their eyes glued to reality TV often make choices to be big and bold. Striving to make themselves into the people they think others want them to be, they lose more and more of their authentic selves along the way and have an increasingly harder time accessing their true voice. In this process of seeking to impress, they can confuse quantity with quality in their communication and embarrass themselves and you in their pursuit to stand out and be noticed. I know. I've done it.

When I first started building my coaching business, I so desperately wanted everyone to like—and quite honestly work with me—that my initial introduction was about 45 seconds during which I didn't take a breath. Or do much pleasing. *"Hi, my name is Alexia Vernon and I am a career and leadership coach and trainer. I use a praxis-centered model for learning and development to empower educators, nonprofit professionals, artists, creatives, and people in a myriad of other helping professions to achieve personal and professional transformation. I work with individuals and organizations who are looking to get to their next level of success and social impact."* There are so many problems with that intro, yet I feel compelled to at least outline the top three. Number one: I'm speaking about how I do what I do and who I do it for with minimal attention given to outcome. Horrible marketing! Number two: I sound equal parts analytical and arrogant. Number three: I know nothing about the person I'm speaking with so I can't possibly connect. Fortunately, I realized all of this before my burgeoning business went belly-up. Now when I introduce myself, depending on the group, you're lucky if I'll get out an entire sentence before asking a series of questions to really get to know who I'm speaking with.

After your young professionals no longer feel like they have to tread water and can start swimming with some abandon, be on the lookout for any desire to perform cannonballs. Overplanning what to say in meetings and taking bathroom breaks whenever senior leadership is schmoozing by the water cooler are telltale signs. Intervene before overtalking and people-pleasing become habit. Remember too that your young professionals likely sat in classrooms from kindergarten through college where classroom participation factored highly into their grades. Quantity rather than quality was often measured. Laud your young professionals when they communicate in a way that moves a conversation forward and supports the achievement of results. Gently identify when they are speaking to fill dead air, and help them identify the impulse that triggered their nonessential communication. Support them to make a different choice when that impulse comes up in the future, and with enough practice, soon it won't.

One of my favorite questions to share with groups prone to excessive talking is "Why Am I Talking?" or WAIT. It's such a simple question, and when one is able to make the process of asking it of one's self a habit, the other habit of shooting one's mouth off is easily corrected. When young professionals understand that listening and connecting with an audience is equally if not more important than seizing face time—something we'll look at in more depth in chapter 8—they will use their speech more efficiently and effectively.

Another equally toxic and related communication habit to nip in the bud should it appear is what my father calls "puffing." He used to joke that my first boyfriend was a "puffer," and no, it's not what you think. Every time I would bring my beau over for dinner, my dad would shoot me knowing glances as the guy, bless him, tried to impress my dad with stories of how he was best friends in high school with such and such celebrity and had turned down a football scholarship to a Pac–10 school to focus more on his studies at a liberal arts school. That he had since dropped out of.

This puffing of the truth comes from the same impulse as talking excessively. While I can't share with you as snazzy of an acronym as WAIT to introduce and tenderly use with your young professionals, I will offer you a mantra that you can feel free to pull out of your pocket as necessary—"Who I Am Is Not What I Achieve." Remind young professionals who place too much stock on outward success that "who" they are runs deeper than how much money they save—or make, depending on their role—your company. It's not about title. It's not about whether they get featured in your company newsletter or in the paper. It is about the choices they make in their thinking and behavior and the results they achieve. This will support them to be true with their communication, and of course to use it to forward organizational goals.

MAKE NOT HAVING AN ANSWER AN ACCEPTABLE ANSWER

DAY 1

While this in many ways is a caveat to the tactic before, it's so important in developing top-notch talent I've chosen to let it stand alone. When you have employees like your young professionals who have been bred and groomed like prize horses for competition, have them experience as soon as possible what it's like *not* to regurgitate their ideas 24/7 as early as possible. Encourage young professionals *not* to run with the first idea that pops into their noggin and to consider a range of possibilities—before speaking or taking action. Remove the pressure that arises when not knowing what to do or how to respond—that has likely become habit over years of development—by removing the stakes attached to being right or making a choice.

Letting young professionals feel safe dancing a little in the unknown is different than encouraging them to let fear paralyze them from doing anything at all. Mastering this tactic is about creating a balance between the presumption of needing to take action immediately (and often incorrectly) to the contrasting, equally unproductive behavior of thinking oneself into a labyrinth of confusion and self-doubt. To strike this delicate balance with your young professionals, encourage them to approach information they are hearing, reading, or in any other way considering through three lenses: *What do I know with my head? What do I know with my heart? What do I know with my gut?* In those rare cases where there is alignment between knowledge (practical, educational, and experiential), the way they feel, and gut instinct, that's when they can answer pretty promptly. However, when there is either misalignment between the three or one area isn't evoking an answer, encourage them to identify what they need to discover before taking action and how they will know when they're ready to do it.

Let's imagine that a young professional, Josh, is a loan officer trying to get a couple closed and into a new home. His bank has issued the couple conditional approval so they went ahead and put down an offer—which was accepted—and now the rep at the seller's bank is telling Josh he needs to get the couple ready to close in 14 days or the deal won't go through. In his head, Josh is saying that this is impossible. He needs at least another month to straighten out the couple's new dent in their credit and to compile a new round of letters from the couple's employers. In his heart, Josh wants to see his clients happy and believes that they can afford the home. His gut is a bit like a 4th of July fireworks show. What should he do?

The answer is as simple and nuanced as the question to Lindsey Pollak's communication scenario in the first tactic of the chapter. *It depends.* Most young professionals in Josh's position want to tell the seller's bank rep "yes" or "no" on the phone and just move on. Ambiguity, particularly in high-stress situations, isn't desired. Josh is lucky enough to be managed by somebody reading this book, so he knows that he first needs to check in with his head, heart, and gut. Seeing both misalignment and missing information, he identifies what he needs to know—what his broker will ultimately need to either say "yay" or "nay" to the loan. Only then can he tell the seller's rep whether it's worth trying for the tight close or walking away. With this information clear, Josh can now tell the seller's rep he'll get back to her in the next day and schedule some time with his broker to see if even though he's got some missing pieces, he'll be able to sign off on the loan.

DEVELOP STRONG AND SUCCINCT PRESENTATION SKILLS

As we've explored in the last few tactics, keen communication stems from keen critical thinking. When young professionals can identify and articulate how they know what they know, they set themselves up to be heard and respected. Nowhere is this commitment to critical thinking more important than in presenting. While we often think of presenting as giving a formal speech or running a meeting, communication situations your young professionals may or may not find themselves in, one is really a presenter any time she opens her mouth and expects someone to listen and take action based on her message.

I'm not audacious enough to propose I can share with you everything you want to impart to young professionals about effectively presenting their ideas. From this chapter you already have some key tactics—work backward to formulate what one will say, support opinions with evidence, make content audience-appropriate, use connectives to show the relationship between ideas, and deploy stop-and-smile any time one loses her place. There are five additional key ingredients to effective presenting. First, it's important for young professionals to understand that any time they want someone to take action from their ideas, they need to be persuasive. Too often speakers of all ages share features and benefits about their topic, yet they fail to make the case for why it's important to take action now.

One of my favorite structures for presenting is plucked from my communication professor days, and it's called Monroe's Motivated Sequence.

 Monroe's Motivated Sequence is particularly useful when everyone in an audience agrees that there is a problem and speakers want to show that their idea is the best one. When your young professionals use this format, they are able to make an emotional connection with their audience. Just like I hope they will whenever they want to get their point across, they organize their thinking by working backward from their **call to action**. In this structure, just beforehand, presenters plan out what is called the **visualization**. They show what their solution to the problem looks like when it's employed. As they continue to work backward, the part they plan next is the **satisfaction**. In this section, presenters identify and describe exactly what the solution looks like. Prior to the satisfaction, speakers build simpatico with whomever they are speaking by describing the **need**. They show an audience that they get it, and by doing so they build rapport and credibility. And finally, they work themselves backward to the beginning of their presentation. In Monroe's Motivated Sequence, the primary purpose here is to gain **attention**.

Second, in their desire to be taken seriously, those young professionals who are attuned to earning respect and demonstrating their know-how can often be boring when they share their ideas. Remind them of the importance of being authentic and personable when they present. Whether that means inserting jokes that are audience-appropriate and allowing for a good laugh at nobody's expense, modulating their voices to hold interest, or telling a good and relevant story, support developing employees to be equal parts professional and engaging.

Third, it's important for young professionals to understand the impact of their body language on their audience. When people don't do a lot of face-to-face communication they can become easily disconnected from the messages they send when they fail to make eye contact, keep their arms crossed and hands planted in their pits, or stick one foot in front of the other as they speak. Show them how to command a room by standing hip width distance apart with a slight bend to their knees, both feet planted firmly on the ground. Teach them to communicate confidence and credibility by imagining they have a string running through their bodies—one side rooting them into the earth and the other pulling them nice and tall toward the sky. Encourage the appropriate use of gesturing—to help take a message from oneself to an audience. To this end, make sure that when they are not deliberately using their hands they are out of pockets, off of hips, and placed by one's side. Remind them that the most important gesturing they can do is with their eyes. Eye contact is a piece of this. Really seeing the people they speak with is another.

Fourth, it's important to choose visual aids that enhance rather than distract from your point. A lot of young professionals rely too much on technology when presenting their ideas. PowerPoint slides contain paragraphs of information rather than some simple pictures, quotes, or statistics that draw out their main and supporting points. When this happens, young professionals wind up delivering their content to their computer and audience members wind up staring at a screen rather than at the presenter. In addition to helping young professionals use A/V the right way, remind them when it's appropriate to hand out materials—either before or after their presentation. That way they don't have people ruffling through papers while they're speaking and disengaging.

Finally, train young professionals to identify and be ready to handle questions and objections that are likely to arise. This will help them both to touch upon these hot buttons during their presentation and to be ready for resistance that might arise. Teach young professionals to keep their cool during a challenge, answer a question to the best of their ability, and remind the questioning party of the evidence they have that backs up their claim. Many times young professionals will not know the answer to a question, particularly when they are still in their first 90 days. Remind them to own this when it happens, find the answer, and get it to the person who wants it.

The key to taking young professionals from mediocre to marvelous in their communication—be it face-to-face or presentational—is identifying what good communication looks like and then ensuring you take the time to build the skills that are necessary to make it happen. This needs to be a major part of your onboarding process. If you allow young professionals to foster and solidify bad communication habits or address communication in a one-off training, you are repeating the mistakes made in primary, secondary, and higher education we explored at the start of the chapter. You are setting yourself up to be disappointed by your young professional and setting that young professional up to under deliver on expectations. No matter how much communication skills training happens formally, this is one of the most important areas for young professionals' direct supervisors to follow up on. Ensure that they are armed with the simple and effective techniques that empower young professionals to speak with confidence and competence each time they open their mouths.

Tweet-Sized Takeaways

- Distinguish communication preference from style, and have young professionals share theirs and learn their team's.

- Identify key categories of people young professionals interact with and make clear what is appropriate for each.

- Discuss communication preferences for each of the four generations in the workplace and devise adaptation strategies.

- Teach young professionals to back up their arguments with unbiased, relevant evidence.

- Before sharing their ideas, have young professionals plot out what they want to say by developing ideas backward from a call to action.

- Stop vocalized thinking by helping young professionals slow down, end their sentences, and use the "stop-and-smile."

- Train young professionals to make nice with connectives.

- Empower young professionals to connect first and speak second. Encourage honest, heart-centered communication.

- Make it okay *not* to have an answer as long as one owns up to it and figures out what information is missing.

- Develop effective presentation skills for young professionals' diverse formal and informal presentations.

chapter 6:

Ensure a Return on Your Expectations

"For, he that expects nothing shall not be disappointed, but he that expects much—if he lives and uses that in hand day by day—shall be full to running over."

Edgar Cayce

If I had a dollar to invest for every time a manager has told me, "I hated to do it, but I had to let _____ go" or "I had to put _____ on probation," I'd have one robust Roth IRA by now. While I've elicited more than a few scowls by replying to such statements with a somewhat bemused, "What was your role in that failure?," the question has always been genuine. In our companies—as well as our schools and our families—there is an epidemic of viewing underperformance or shattered expectations as the fault of one person. Unfortunately, this is rarely the case. It takes two hardworking partners to build a successful marriage, a tribe to raise and educate a child, and an active partnership between a company's HR department, learning and development arm, and a young professional's direct supervisor to get that young professional successfully to the end of her first 90 days. Once we understand that we are as responsible for the success of a new hire as the new hire herself, then and only then can we learn, apply, and refine the key strategies for ensuring our young professionals get to where they need to be.

If you want greatness from your young professionals—and surely you do or you wouldn't be reading this book—you want to inspire it from day one. You do this by communicating clearly what greatness looks like when it's in full bloom, and you ensure that your new hires understand your definition. You plant the seed for greatness by speaking about your company/department/team as an incubator for the best and brightest people, ideas, and projects. And most importantly, you observe how your young professionals are growing and you shift your strategy based on what you observe—and what they tell you—they need.

In one of my favorite books on collaborative leadership, *As One*, authors Mehrdad Baghai and James Quigley use the relationship between a senator and citizens—as conceived and played out by the Ancient Romans—as an archetype to describe a way for leaders to elicit the best from their employees. According to Baghai and Quigley, "Citizens are filled with the notion of freedom and pride in their work. Their behaviors are guided by the constitution and by their strong sense of belonging, thus they work hard to ensure that the community and what it represents are preserved. Equally important, senators help create an environment where citizens can make autonomous decisions. No one tells them what choices to make; they understand how their decisions impact the overall success of the community."

This is an effective way to think about how to engender success from young new hires. Our newest generation of workplace professionals grew up in a self-help culture that has suggested they are entitled to and have a responsibility to derive meaning from their professional work. As we have explored, our new young professionals have been working collaboratively from the time they were in preschool and are used to thinking about what best serves the needs and desires of a group. While this generation has been stereotyped as coddled, its members are used to having a voice in the decisions that affect them and the rest of their team or "community." As companies, when we can follow Baghai and Quigley's charge to provide a "constitution" with principles and values for which young professionals can operate and measure their success by, then we can "step back and allow the citizens to come to decisions on their own."

Return-on-Investment (ROI) Vs. Return-on-Expectations (ROE)

When we measure **ROI**, we are looking to measure the success of the "investment" (the money, time, and energy) we have made in an employee's learning and growth. While plenty of metrics exist to capture how effective onboarding drives business results by reducing turnover, inefficiency, mistakes, and so forth—I believe that attempting to measure your **ROE**, particularly around onboarding, is a more effective means for assessing success and strengthening your practices. *What do you expect employees to be able "to do" by the end of their 90 days? Make 40 sales calls per day? Receive good to excellent ratings on "smiley sheets" after each of their weekly presentations?* When you are able to answer how success will be achieved for your young professionals—and ultimately for yourself—you will be able to develop an onboarding action plan that gets your expectations met. You will also ensure that HR, training, and management are all cogs that are part of the same wheel: new hire success.

BE TRANSPARENT

Transparency is one of the key catalysts for sustainable workplace success. As we explored in chapter 3, this generation of young professionals thrives with a syllabus. They like to know what they are responsible for (chief responsibilities and accountabilities), when key assignments are due (project deadlines), and how grades will be determined (means for assessment).

Transparency makes a great workplace core value. And companies with honest and accessible customer and employee reviews, pay scales, and promotion pathways consistently report higher profitability, employee engagement, and retention. Transparency is equally important when it comes to employee expectations, particularly for young new hires. Let your new hires know what you expect, and make yourself a partner in helping them get there.

While HR and training want to set their expectations during their first touch with a new hire, if you are a manager or direct supervisor, your initial conversation about your expectations for your young professional should happen by the end of the first week. During this conversation, you want to clarify exactly what you expect from your new hire in each of the following P's. Questions to ask yourself in order to help you identify the exact pieces you want to convey include:

Professionalism

(Note: Some of these you may have addressed prior to the first day. However, it's not a bad idea to revisit them again.)

- What is appropriate workplace dress?

- What is the appropriate use of technology, particularly social media?

- Can employees take personal calls in the workplace?

- What kind of relationship can young professionals enjoy with managers outside of the workplace?

- Can colleagues date? If so, must they be in different departments? Have lateral positions? Report the romance to HR?

Performance

- What are the three to five key indicators of outstanding performance in this position?

- What skills and behaviors do you want to see evidence of?

- What are key benchmarks in performance that must be met in the first 90 days?

- What are key project deadlines that must be hit in the first 90 days?

- How are promotions and raises decided?

Problem Solving

- What are proven best practices for handling the "typical" problems that someone in this role will encounter?

- How should a young professional navigate a problem? At what point should a supervisor be brought in?

- What are company practices for handling internal conflict or conflict with a customer/stakeholder should it emerge?

Passion

- What's an appropriate workplace attitude?

- What values do successful employees carry into their work?

- How can young professionals demonstrate creativity and innovation?

- How can new hires best incorporate themselves within (while actively shaping) company culture?

The way you frame conversations about expectations is just as important as communicating what you expect. By asking yourself the questions above, you will undoubtedly hit upon company and individual policies and procedures for which there is no wiggle room. *At Doug's Doodads we have a zero-tolerance policy for violence in the workplace. We define violence as the physical, sexual, verbal, or emotional abuse of an employee, customer, or stakeholder.* Fair enough. Yet I suspect your company (and particularly you) have a lot of "soft" expectations, particularly in the areas of attitude, engagement, problem solving, and innovation for which there are not clear guidelines or means for assessment. These areas—what I like to call the "connective tissue"—will determine whether your young professionals will have the muscle, strength, and endurance to stay running (for while 90 days will get them ready for the race, ultimately it's a marathon and not a sprint). As we will next explore, if we want a champion athlete or star performer, we need the person in question to be a pivotal part of designing the action plan.

CO-CREATE MEANS FOR ASSESSMENT

DAY 7

In conjunction with articulating your expectations in as much detail as possible, you want to discuss how you will measure achievement in each of the four Ps. To obtain buy-in to your expectations and create the foundation necessary for a young professional not only to meet but also to exceed expectations, solicit their ideas for how success will be measured. To return to our previous metaphor, get clear on what your young professional or "athlete" needs to stay hydrated, flexible, strong, and fast.

Some key questions to ask are:

• How can I best support you in achieving _____?

- What is the balance between structure and freedom you need to consistently give your best?

- How are you best able to listen to and incorporate feedback?

- What kind of formal and informal assessment has previously worked well for you?

- What are the things I should avoid doing at all costs that you know shut you down and impede success?

Strive to show up to conversations with the sole agenda of co-creating a viable, results-oriented plan and follow-up strategy. Ensure that you are asking questions that facilitate insight for your employees, particularly young new hires who thrive in such a learner-centered environment. By doing so, your job becomes easier and your employees will achieve greater success—for they will have taken ownership over their own learning.

FIND YOUR EMPLOYEE'S MOTIVATORS

DAY 7

In one of my favorite books on motivation, *Drive*, author Daniel Pink differentiates between extrinsic and intrinsic motivators and provides numerous recommendations for how leaders, managers, and companies can and should shift from the former to the latter. He suggests that if the overall work that your young professional new hire is engaging in is in any way stimulating, creative, and requires autonomy, consistently relying on carrots to drive performance and results ultimately yields one of these "Seven Deadly Flaws":

- They can extinguish intrinsic motivation.

- They can diminish performance.

- They can crush creativity.

- They can crowd out good behavior.

- They can encourage cheating, shortcuts, and unethical behavior.

- They can become addictive.

- They can foster short-term thinking.

To understand how to hook into intrinsic motivators to catalyze an employee's drive, it's important to again reference Pink and draw an important distinction between motivation and inspiration.

 ## Motivation Vs. Inspiration

Motivation is the individual force within a person that makes her want to show up to life at 100 percent to perform at 100 percent. **Inspiration**, on the other hand, is what draws out a person's motivation. As managers, trainers, coaches, or consultants, we cannot motivate someone. Something is either a motivator for someone or it is not. What we can do is identify what specifically motivates each of our employees and step into the role of inspirer by enabling our people to harness their motivators in their work.

While as you know I'm not a big fan of stereotypes, I do think it's important to understand what members of each generation typically value most, so that we as workplace managers and leaders can harness this enthusiasm to produce the results we seek. As I've shared with you previously, our current generation of young professionals particularly values work where they feel like they are making a positive social and environmental impact, the ability to learn and grow in their workplaces, and the ability to achieve integration between work and life. They also like to be acknowledged in front of others for exemplary work. In other words, it's not the trophy. It's the ceremony where they receive the trophy that matters!

Therefore, consider how to inspire your young professionals via peer recognition. Sodexo is one company that has figured out how to do this well. Sodexo's brand ambassadors participate in the Brand Ambassador of the Month (BAM!) program. While the person who has done the best job promoting Sodexo in their online communities is simply recognized on the team call, Senior Director of Talent Acquisition, Sherie Valderrama, says that peer recognition does an incredibly powerful job of tapping her staff's desire to be honored. "When we announce the winner on a team call," Sherie explains, "that person doesn't just receive congratulations on the phone. It's not uncommon for 40 tweets to go out from the Sodexo community in a matter of minutes acknowledging the person. That goes a long way with our people."

Remember too that motivators will also be shaped by the industry you are in. For example, in the leadership and career development program I lead for new nurses, approximately 80 percent of each cohort I work with—irrespective of hospital or specialization—report that feeling competent is one of their biggest motivators to staying engaged in their work. When I have worked with other groups of young professionals, such as MBA students or new business associates, one of the motivators I typically encounter is the ability to create solutions for problems people have previously put up with.

There is no surefire recipe for sourcing your young professionals' motivators. You can have them do one of the many motivation styles assessments that exist. You can have them identify the times in their life they have been most motivated by the academic, philanthropic, or professional work they were doing and have them explore common themes that were present. And most importantly—and most simply—you can ask. *What gets you most jazzed? What can I do to help you harness your motivation in the work that you do?* Or if you suspect there is some barrier getting in the way—particularly as you creep into your second or third month of work together, a time when the initial walking on egg shells to impress and people please stops—*What barriers are getting in the way of you feeling motivated? How can we partner together to remove them?* Then, make sure you are applying this information in how you are assigning work to your young professionals: checking in and holding them accountable; acknowledging them when they have been successful; troubleshooting with them when they get stuck; and pushing them to the next level of success when they are ready for a new challenge. Not sure how to solve all of those potential challenges? This question does have an answer. And it's coaching.

CREATE A COACHING CULTURE

DAY 14

As we have explored so far in the onboarding tactics in this chapter, whether you are looking to create a system for assessment or learning how to identify your young professional's motivators, the key to having conversations that lead to results is to coach. While I'm a bit uncomfortable privileging one onboarding tactic over another, if you were to play with only one of our 90, this would without a doubt be the tactic I'd want you to use. For when new hires are open to being coached and can apply it, together there really is no problem that cannot be bulldozed through.

While there are as many different definitions of coaching and approaches to doing it as there are people who profess to coach, we're going to explore what I have found to be the most simple way to conceptualize coaching. Then, we will look at how to do it as effortlessly, efficiently, and consistently as possible with your new young professionals.

 Coaching is a confidential, empowering, and catalytic relationship between a coach and coachee(s) to facilitate learning and growth, improve performance, and close the gap from where coachee(s) are to where they aspire to be.

When someone steps into the role of coach, she begins by establishing that the conversation is confidential and then seeks to learn as much as possible about where the person receiving the coaching is coming from. To be successful as a coach, whether coaching a young professional or a senior leader, one must let go of an agenda for the person receiving coaching, use curiosity to ask questions that promote critical thinking and insight, listen to what is being said (and not said), and adapt her approach to best fit the needs of who is being coached. Coaching conversations are often scheduled to allow the person receiving coaching to show up as prepared as possible, yet they can be impromptu as long as both parties are game. Because young professionals tend to be adaptable, multitasking, and comfortable with real-time feedback due to their immersion in online media, they are the generation perhaps most amenable to impromptu coaching.

For coaching to yield results, the coach must enable the person receiving coaching to define the focus of the conversation as early as possible. This is pivotal, particularly for young professionals who may not be familiar with coaching. For those new to receiving coaching, it can be tricky to identify what the goal is and it can be easy to get wrapped up in story. For example, while your new hire might need to vent for a few minutes about her overwhelming feelings, you both will have a more productive conversation if she can identify that she would like to walk away with a couple of strategies to improve time management. Other times the focus will be somewhat ephemeral—getting comfortable in one's new role. When the coachee identifies a focus without clear means for assessing whether the goal has been met, a coach wants to unpick the aim. *How will you know when you are comfortable? What will being comfortable look and feel like to you? What will be the payoff?*

Once an agenda is created, the coach asks questions to help coachee(s) tap into their own wisdom and find the answers to get them where they want to go. You should resist the temptation to take answers at face value, knowing that people often see symptoms of problems rather than their sources. Therefore, your questions should push coachees beyond their own assumptions and help them explore possibilities they may have never previously considered. Just as importantly, you help people see themselves as creators of their own experiences. Even when people don't like the choices before them, a choice always exists—even if it's simply about how to process and archive an experience. Here are some effective questions for your coaching toolbox:

Getting Unstuck

- If you knew the answer, how would it begin?

- What are you pretending not to know?

- How can you remove the pressure of getting "the right" answer so that you are open to recognizing *your* answer?

- How can I support you in brainstorming some possibilities?

- What would choosing the path of least resistance look like?

Empowering

- Where have you been successful?

- What's your role in this?

- Who are you called to *be* in this situation?

- How might this be an opportunity for you to play "a bigger game"?

- Who will you be as a result of this achievement?

Thinking About Your Own Thinking

- How long have you been thinking about this?

- If you were to look at _____ as a symptom of something deeper, what could be its source?

- If _____ keeps showing up, what does this suggest about what you are putting out into the world?

- How can you shift this obstacle into an opportunity?

- What's the lesson you are ready to learn, once and for all?

During a coaching conversation—which usually lasts 20–45 minutes—you dance between asking questions, mirroring back what you are picking up, and devising action. As a coach you are never telling someone else what to do. You may share best practices you have seen work, or offer up your own ideas when brainstorming. For learning to stick and facilitate shifts in thinking, behavior, and results, coachees need to settle on their own answers and articulate what they will do with the content of the conversation.

Therefore, it's incredibly important as a coach to bring a coaching conversation to a close by allowing the person receiving coaching to share back what has been most useful from the conversation and how she will apply it moving forward. As we will explore in more detail in our next tactic on feedback, you also want to be clear on follow-up, assessment, and how you can support the achievement of results. This can all be accomplished in a few simple questions. *Tell me, what are you taking away from our conversation? What has been most useful for you about what we've explored?* Once the person has sufficiently answered, then you can follow up with a question or two about next steps. *How will you transfer what you are taking away into action? How can I support you in meeting these objectives?* Let's take a look at how to apply these coaching principles in real world practice.

In the following scenario, "Nurse Nancy" is finishing her fourth week as a new nurse on the medical-surgical floor of an urban hospital. Like most recent graduates, Nancy is being paired with a preceptor—a veteran nurse who is sharing her patient load with Nancy and helping her learn everything she needs to know about her role, before flying solo at the end of her first six to eight weeks on the job. For those unfamiliar with current nursing culture, a new nurse grad can expect to work three to four 12-hour shifts per week, carry a patient load of initially two, and eventually up to six patients. And on a med-surg floor where most new nurses land, they will spend the majority of a shift on their feet, running between patient rooms, making phone calls to doctors, consulting with families, and learning new technology and charting systems. Many of these new nurses don't get a break. Many also rotate between day, night, and graveyard shifts, meaning they may not be able to sleep between shifts and are showing up to work tired.

In the role play we're going to explore, Nancy's preceptor, Paula, has noticed that Nancy is no longer the bright-eyed, overeager, perfectionist nurse she was paired with a month earlier. She's not sure what is going on with Nancy, but she is worried about her—and of course how her changes in attitude and energy might be shifting her behavior. Already she's noticed that one of her charts had too much explanation (nurses are asked to chart by exception) and that some of her words were unclearly abbreviated. Let's see how Paula, a skilled coach, is able to help her new hire unpick what has been going on and explore ways to move from grad to great—following the best coaching practices we detailed in the previous pages.

 ### Preceptor Paula Coaches Nurse Nancy

Paula: Nancy, thank you so much for taking a moment to chat with me. Is this still a good time? (1)

Nancy: Absolutely. It feels really good to get off my feet.

Paula: Yes, I think it's fair to say we're both pretty exhausted. Tell me. How has your day been going?

Nancy: All right, I guess.

Paula: What have been your high points of the shift? (2)

Nancy: I feel like I've been doing a good job balancing my time between patients.

Paula: I agree. Your time management skills have definitely grown in the last few days. (3) What strategies have enabled you to do this? (4)

Nancy: Taking a few minutes at the start of my shift to map out what I need to get done and the best order to do it all in. Also, dividing tasks into short-term urgent, long-term urgent, short-term non-urgent, and long-term non-urgent has really helped. I used to never get to any long-term non-urgent, and now I make sure I slip these in once I've gotten the short-term urgent tasks taken care of.

Paula: This is terrific, Nancy. I'm really impressed. (5)

Nancy: That means a lot. Sometimes I feel like I'm not really working at my best. I have a tendency to repeat in my head everything I've done wrong and never remember anything I did that was right.

Paula: I'm not sure I know what you mean. I see a lot of potential in you. Could you tell me a little bit more about that? (6)

Nancy: I've just been second-guessing myself a lot lately. That's actually why I've been wanting to talk to you. I'm sure you've noticed. I don't feel like I'm the same person I showed up as a few weeks back. I don't know how to get back to my old self, and I really want to.

Paula: Is that what you'd like to walk away with today? A plan for getting back to your "old self?" (7)

Nancy: That would be amazing if that could happen. Yes.

Paula: When you think about your "old self," who do you see? (8)

Nancy: That's a good question. I guess it's less about seeing. I mean sure, I had a smile on my face. I couldn't wait to get to work. But more than anything, I just felt like I was prepared for this experience. I wasn't in this alone.

Paula: What has gotten in the way of you feeling like you have a team to turn to when you are unsure of an answer or need some verification? (9)

Nancy: I guess it happened after Sarah [the charge nurse on the floor] heard me reading an incorrect dose to a doctor on the phone. She pulled the phone out of my hand, told the doctor I had made a mistake, and since then I've just felt like I was walking on eggshells around her. Kind of around everyone. I haven't wanted to ask for help. I keep making mistakes. And a lot of days I just feel like I'm an idiot. And it's becoming somewhat of a self-fulfilling prophecy. Now, I'm getting sloppy with my own charts. I know better than that. I just can't shake the feeling that I disappointed Sarah. And now, everyone else.

Paula: I can tell that thinking you've let someone else down is really hard for you. How might forgiving *yourself* start a chain reaction of positive results in this situation? (10)

Nancy: It would be huge. I would be able to get out of my head, stay in the moment, stop making such careless mistakes, and just feel better overall. I'd also probably be able to sleep better when I finally make it to bed.

Paula: How will you make this commitment to yourself—once and for all? (11)

Nancy: When I hear my inner critic pop up, I'm going to remind myself that I am a smart and capable nurse. I literally just need to repeat that to myself again and again until that message sticks. And I can ask myself, "What did I do right today?" The more I put my attention to that, the more I will keep doing things more and more right.

Paula: How can you apply what you have learned with Sarah moving forward? (12)

Nancy: Oh my goodness, not be embarrassed to ask for another set of eyes to read over something if I'm at all unsure. I will ask for help when I need it. And if I do make a mistake, I'm going to own it in the moment and not let myself wilt. You know, until we started talking about this I don't think I even realized how this one incident has seriously undermined me almost every day for the last few weeks. I realize now that if I could have just said, "Sarah, I'm sorry for misreading the number. Thank you for having my back," I would have felt like I stepped into my power rather than away from it. And I think that's the key to me feeling competent. Standing tall in difficult situations rather than shrinking from them.

Paula: You are a powerful person, Nancy. When you believe that, your enthusiasm and ability to make a difference are infectious. We're here for you. You just have to let us know how we can help. Now, I know we need to get back out on the floor, so let's start to bring everything we've talked about together. What has been of most value to you during our conversation today? (13)

Nancy: Having the space to talk this all out. Like I said, I knew that I wasn't myself but I really wasn't sure why. Recognizing that the way I store an experience is as important as the experience itself is a really big "aha" for me. Also, learning how to stop myself in the midst of a negative thought pattern. And of course, making the commitment to reach out to my team. You all are here for me.

Paula: How can I best support you in applying what you learned today? (14)

Nancy: When we have our check-ins, it would be really great if you could just ask me how my inner critic is doing. Also, I'm going to pay attention to my charting. Make sure that when I'm doing it, I'm really focused on my writing. No more abbreviations or unnecessary explanations. If you could look at my next few and tell me how they look, that would be really useful.

Paula: You got it, Nancy. I can't wait to see how you continue to evolve in our next few weeks together. I think your future is very bright. (15)

The Core Pieces of the Coaching Conversation

(1) Asking for permission

(2) Asking a possibility-centered question to empower

(3) Mirroring back success

(4) Facilitating learning and growth

(5) More affirmation

(6) Asking for clarification

(7) Setting agenda

(8) Facilitating learning and growth

(9) Listening to what is not being said

(10) Facilitating learning and growth; moving to action

(11) Facilitating learning and growth; moving to action

(12) Facilitating learning and growth; moving to action

(13) Recapping

(14) Next Steps

(15) Empowering

DO IT EARLY...AND OFTEN

DAY 21

No, believe it or not I'm not talking about voting. I'm talking about feedback. Unless you are the head of the Institute of Psychic Arts and your new hires are all recent grads from your academic program, they need to know how they are performing beyond semiannual or quarterly reviews, and certainly before their first 90 days are up. After all, if it takes 90–120 days to create a new habit, you want to reinforce productive behaviors and curb the not-so-productive ones as early as possible.

In a recent whitepaper, "The Future of Millennial Careers," Millennial business and workplace expert Alexandra Levit reports: "51 percent of managers believe Millennials exhibit an inability to accept criticism from their managers" and "54 percent of Millennials are in agreement." In order to break through this potential barrier to young professional new hire success, you want to be able to have your new hires identify their own gaps in thinking or performance through the kind of coaching conversation we explored between Preceptor Paula and Nurse Nancy. These kinds of questions enable you to set your new hire up to engage in the thinking, self-reflection, and action planning necessary to meet and hopefully exceed your expectations. When your new hires can identify their own blind spots and areas for improvement, they are far more likely to self-correct and take your direct feedback when you do offer it.

Sometimes, even when you approach feedback from a coaching perspective, you don't get to the place you intended. Let's assume you have let go of the assumption that what you have been witnessing with your new hire is the source of the problem rather than the symptom. You created a safe space for exploration. You empowered your young professional. And she just isn't getting it. Or lacks the knowledge or skill necessary to create a new habit in thinking or behavior. You need to deliver some feedback.

As I hope you would with any of your other employees, make sure you set a time to talk that is mutually agreed upon. If you want them to be in a space where they can let down their guard, truly listen to what you have to say, and take action from it, then they need to consent to having the talk and engage in it at a time when and where they can be fully present.

The most important thing you can do for your young professional is to stay in the coach zone. Even if questions like *How would you evaluate your performance over the last week?* elicit a blank stare—or even worse, unwarranted self-praising—resist the temptation to go into telling mode. Keep your recommendations rooted in specifics and behaviors. Keep the emotion out of it.

If Nurse Nancy in our previous coaching conversation had never brought up her sloppy charting or had not had the problem with her charge nurse and simply was underperforming, you can use an observation as an entry point into your feedback. *I've noticed that you are no longer charting by exception and that there have been some mistakes in your documentation.* Stick to the facts. Give the statement a moment to land and sink in. Then, follow up with a question in the way that a young professional can best hear it. If you have a casual relationship, perhaps it's, *So tell me, Nancy, what's been going on?* Listen to what Nancy has to say, and articulate as clearly as possible the behavior you need her to exhibit and its significance—in whatever order makes the most sense. *Nancy, as I know you know, charting is vital for keeping a patient's entire team on the same page and for ensuring patient safety. Moving forward, can I count on you to spell each word out—no more abbreviations—and to repeat back to a doctor anything you are hearing on the phone before writing it down?* To which, if Nancy wants to keep her job—I kid, somewhat— she will surely say, "yes." You are now on the same page. The behavioral change is clear and actionable.

In addition to having timely conversations, asking for permission, being specific, and keeping the focus on the behavior you want to solidify (or reshape), you also want to keep your feedback the right kind of personal. Also, ensure that there's a follow-up plan attached to it. For example, if you know that a young new hire is working on weeding out the kind of vocalized thinking we discussed in the previous chapter, rather than bombard her with feedback on every realm of her face-to-face communication, give her a suggestion such as "stop-and-smile." Explain how to apply it to eliminate her favorite filler phrase, "so you know." Then, after you devise a strategy for the behavioral modification, co-create the plan for follow-up. Again, if possible, elicit your young professional in the solution. *I love that you want to get comfortable with stop-and-smile. How will you practice it in the next two weeks before we have a conversation check-in?*

Action planning is vital. If you feel like you are receiving a wishy-washy response, clarify further. *I appreciate that you are going to use stop-and-smile in workplace conversations. Let's distill that down further so that we are both clear how that looks in action. I'm giving you the challenge to practice stop-and-smile with each member of our sales team in the next 14 days. That way you are using it with people who are familiar with the exercise and who can support you by giving you reminders if you should lapse back into the "so you knows."*

And most importantly, if you want to facilitate follow-through, link action items to what your young professionals care about. Suzy Rogers, an HR manager for Rockwell Automation, does this well. One technique she uses is to craft analogies that speak directly to the interests of her young staff. If she's seeking to reinforce the importance of flexing communication style to meet people where they're at, she might say, "Now imagine that you just purchased your first house. You have a favorite room that you've done up just the way you like, but sometimes you want to go into the other rooms. Now, while you may have a communication style that you go to the most, what can you do to meet people who might be on the other side of the house?"

Suzy also links the feedback she gives to her employees' individual motivators. She describes one young employee as "a goddess of systems"—a real content expert—but in need of developing her ability to coach other staff after being promoted to a new managerial role. Suzy would give her hypothetical scenarios and ask her how she would coach the person in it. Because this young professional was motivated by being perceived as "awesome" in her work, Suzy would recognize her for doing "a good job" in the role plays. And then, she'd push further. "Now, what would it take for you not just to be good, but to be a master? And how can you apply this to next week's scenario?" As Suzy explains, this language really excited her young professional. It also got her to step up her game, and she usually figured out how to do it herself.

BE OPEN TO COACHING

Coachability. The degree that we are open to what the environment can offer or the extent to which we accept and consider input and ideas (Lisa Haneberg, *Coaching Up and Down the Generations*).

To support your young professional in moving efficiently and effectively from new hire to peak performer, make sure that you are willing to step into the role of a coachee and not just the role of a coach. If you follow the recommendations we have played with in the previous pages, you will have successfully modeled how to coach and created the space for your young professionals to give *you* feedback. While you may recognize that this is "good practice," if you are used to a more traditional hierarchal relationship with your employees—particularly those that are new and young—this is going to feel uncomfortable at first. Stick with it.

Remember that your young professionals are part of the first generation that was given permission to provide feedback to their educators and their parents. When they feel like they are builders of their own experiences and not simply passive participants in it, they will know they are in familiar territory. They also will more quickly and creatively move beyond real and self-imposed limitations. They will be able to recognize and ultimately—through self-correction—avoid hiccups in their thinking and behavior. And perhaps most importantly, they will make your job infinitely easier by clarifying how you can help them get to where you both want *them* to be.

Once you get comfortable dancing between the role of coach and coachee, you will notice that your enjoyment of your own role increases. As Lisa Haneberg describes, when you allow yourself to be coached, "You feel a sense of confidence. You are relaxed and feel a professional affection for the other person; after all, she is giving you the gift of time and feedback. And when the feedback is really helpful, you feel a rush of excitement and enthusiasm." Being coachable allows you to move beyond the minutia of a particular situation or mistake and to focus on solutions for moving forward. It allows the person with titular authority to let go of the need to have all of the right answers, and to instead trust that in dialogue you and the other person or people engaged in the coaching conversation hold collective responsibility for future action.

While you can let your new young professionals know that they have permission to give you coaching when you first introduce the practice to them, reinforce your openness after their first month. It will take approximately 30 days for them to know what they need more of, less of, and what is working just right. The more you embrace the key components of creating a coaching culture, the more you will undoubtedly slip back and forth between a coach and a coachee in the course of a conversation.

 ## MAKE MISTAKES TEACHABLE MOMENTS

"'Teachable Moments' are one of the quickest ways to create a learning organization, helping the entire team to learn from the many mistakes on the journey to excellence. The attitude of learning organizations is, if we are going to make mistakes anyway, let's go ahead and learn from them."

Orrin Woodward

You're in the business of facilitating learning and growth if you want employees to perform well, stay engaged, become self-directed, and move to their next level of success. As a generation, our newest young professionals have not been encouraged to take risks. With an increasing emphasis on standardized tests and grade point averages, many young people have been socialized to play it safe and get to "the right answer" as quickly as possible. While I don't believe in regrets, I'm disappointed that I've been such a person. I opted out of several AP classes my last years of high school for fear that I may not receive an A, and as a consequence lower my GPA and not be as competitive for the colleges and scholarships I was applying for. I hope you'll agree with me that you'd rather have a new hire who doesn't get an "A" than a new hire who sets a glass ceiling for her insight and achievement.

Without you creating and modeling a culture where it's okay to take calculated risks and sometimes not deliver on them, your new hires might be good in their roles but they will never be great. In order to institutionalize teachable moments into your new hire's first 90 days—and beyond—begin by asking coaching questions to see if your young professional can identify her mistake on her own. *Karen, I just had a chance to review your first financial report. How do you feel like you did?* If the mistake is either something your young professional wouldn't recognize—for example, not having the amount of funds in her till to match the total transactions you see logged—you may need to begin by identifying the mistake yourself. *Lou, you came up $100 short today. I'd like to talk about what happened.* Then, staying in a coaching frame of mind, identify specifically with your new hire what can be learned from the mistake and how to focus on a lasting solution. If this mistake has happened before, make sure to point this out and tell them you want to know how you can help ensure the mistake is no longer repeated. If your new hire shares that it's a lack of knowledge, fill in the gaps. If it's a breakdown in communication, go back to the strategies you have outlined about communication to speak with rather than at each other moving forward.

Sandwich disappointment over mistakes and broken expectations with positive affirmations rooted in what your new hire is doing well and why she is a valuable member of your team. Ensure that you end such conversations by having her share back what she has learned, how she will tangibly apply this learning moving forward, and what she needs from you to ensure that this is a lesson she never needs to learn again. This ensures that you are truly creating a teachable moment.

UPHOLD CONSEQUENCES

Just as it's important to bring your new hires into the conversation about how they can best meet your expectations, it's important to hold them accountable when they do not. Letting an employee whose skill set, work ethic, or personality is mismatched between role, team, or culture continue on benefits nobody—not you, not that employee, and certainly not the rest of your department or company. If you have been engaged in ongoing coaching and feedback conversations and little to no improvement has been made, the employee you have neglected to hold accountable—as well as future new hires and members of your existing team—will see you as all talk and no action. Knowing that you do not walk your talk, they will begin to push boundaries because they can get away with it. Identify the source of why your new hire is not a fit, and make an appropriate decision for how to take action.

For many employees, a hiccup on the path to success is just that. A hiccup. As discussed in our last tactic, call it out early and set an aggressive plan to fix it. Remember that the first 90 days are meant to be a probationary period. Just like in the criminal justice system, if somebody violates a rule or fails to deliver on a responsibility, your authority and future success necessitates that you implement the consequences—which you hopefully identified and ideally co-created with your new hire as discussed at the start of the chapter.

Here are four common root causes for why effective onboarding may not have created an effective employee, as well as my recommendations for how to address each before the culmination of the first 90 days:

Source	Solution
New hire lacks skills to be successful in the current role.	Provide necessary training and coaching to build skills. If this fails and other relevant skills exist, deploy new hire to a different team or department.
New hire is not adhering to rules or exhibiting appropriate professionalism.	If infractions are minor, place on probation with a detailed, co-created action plan. If problems persist, terminate.
New hire is not in a role where she can play to her strengths.	Identify a different role on the team or in the company for the new hire to fill.
Employee is not a fit with company culture.	Terminate.

REWARD OUTSTANDING PERFORMANCE

DAY 14

To return to Daniel Pink and motivating employees, familiar extrinsic motivators or carrots such as money, title, or benefits can on rare occasion be effective. For example, if a role is inherently not motivating, is short-term, or does not require a lot of deep thinking, then offering familiar carrots like "a dinner certificate for two to each member of the sales team that wins the two-week new member drive" can get employees in gear.

Similarly, if you want to offer an initial one-time incentive to employees who successfully make it to the end of their first 90 days—such as an additional personal day—neither Pink nor I will put you in the Hall of Fame for Most De-Motivating supervisor, trainer, or manager. Remember that if you offer a carrot, you want to point out why you are giving this reward. Perhaps you want to honor that coming in on a Saturday to do a direct mail campaign is tedious, mindless work. Note why the work is necessary and how it will positively make an impact (for example, on you, another department, customers' lives, business results, and so forth).

Use your coaching skills to create awareness and growth for that young professional and to make her increasingly self-directed. *How can you identify if your team needs you again at the 25th hour? How can you tap into your value for service to go beyond your written responsibilities to support the department?* These types of questions will also protect you from developing young professionals who expect something bright and shiny every time they complete a task. And the more adept you become as a coach, the more you will enable your young professionals to see the reward in simply getting their intrinsic motivations honored. When you ask a successful employee, *How does it feel to have met your sales target with two weeks to spare?*, you create the opportunity for her to laud herself for a job well done and to recognize your appreciation of her achievement.

To maximize your ability to get your employees recognized the way that *they* want to be recognized, ask. I recently coached a manager who works with young professionals—many of whom have just earned a two-year degree or are in school and pursuing their bachelor's. "My kids," the manager began. "They just have the worst work ethic. We start them out at $12/hour, we promote them to $15 after their first 90 days, and the minute they get the raise they get super lazy and incredibly chatty with the other representatives. I don't know what to do."

When she asked her employees what most motivated them, perhaps not too surprisingly they didn't say they needed more money or a fancy dinner out, but rather that they wanted to feel like they worked in a more collaborative work environment. My neurons were firing. "How might you incentivize performance by allowing the reps to work together rather than against one another? And if you're going to offer a reward, how can you make it social rather than purely financial?"

A smile began to perk through the manager's previously stiff lips. "Well, I guess we could do a weekly meeting check-in with everyone that wouldn't just be focused on policies and procedures, but instead could function like a roundtable discussion for sharing best practices, challenges, and concerns. And in a month where we as a group meet our target, maybe we could have some kind of social theme for each Friday of the next month—PJ day or dress as your favorite superhero. We could even have a contest where staff members bring in a baby picture from home and each person has to guess who it is from a pile of them."

You probably will not be surprised to learn that although this manager's reps still transitioned out of the company after graduation—which for an entry-level job without a pipeline for advancement is to be expected—employees began to cut out the non-work- related conversation, took ownership over their results, reached out to support and empower team members, and nary a month went by without their "Wacky Fridays." This manager's subtle shift in how she incentivized performance—from external motivation to a strategy that embraced the group's desire for teamwork—transformed an entire culture.

IF IT'S NOT A FIT, LET THEM GO

You've been transparent about your high expectations. You've spent the time to build a relationship with your young professional and to elicit feedback on what motivates her to achieve your vision of success. You've co-created the means for performance assessment. You've used a coaching approach to catalyze performance, followed the best practices set forth for offering actionable feedback, and given your new hire space and permission to share with you how you can best help her. You've held your new hire accountable to the goals that were undertaken. You've been waiting to reward performance but, quite frankly, there has been little to nothing "outstanding" to reward. You've got two choices. You can continue to perpetuate mediocrity. Or you can let your young professional go—on an extended probation, to another department where she is better suited, or, if it's just not a good fit, out the door.

As we explored in the tactic on upholding consequences, nobody benefits from letting under performance continue. It's never any fun letting people go when you have jobs available for them. Yet if you can honestly say to yourself—and to your company— that you are proud of the role you have played in an employee's onboarding and that you did everything in your power to set her up for success, take a deep breath, make sure that the appropriate people are notified and on board with the decision, and then put your plan into action. Then, get back to the provocative work of setting the rest of your young professionals up for success and, as we will explore in the next chapter, get the rest of your employees "focused on their focus."

"Never seem more learned than the people you are with. Wear your learning like a pocket watch and keep it hidden. Do not pull it out to count the hours, but give the time when you are asked."

Lord Chesterfield

As you set out to make the most of your ROE, in addition to facilitating eureka moments for your young professionals, let your young new hires see you take accountability for your mistakes and grow from them. *Did you come up with a proposal for a new company product that promptly got denied because you didn't get all of the key decision makers on board? Did you ever make a client call where you were so eager to close that you misquoted your prices and then had to eat crow afterwards?* Show that you have taken risks and experienced some mighty falls. Explain how this has enabled you to improve your performance and evolve as a professional. Reveal coaching and feedback you have received that has catalyzed your performance. When you demonstrate how you have been knocked down and how you have gotten back up again, your new hires will see the payoff for risk taking. You will help squelch their generational risk aversion. They will see you as a partner and guide to playing a bigger game.

Tweet-Sized Takeaways

- Ensure your ROE by communicating each of the 4 Ps: professionalism, performance, problem solving, and passion.

- Solicit your young professional's ideas for how to hold them accountable.

- Inspire young professionals by identifying what motivates them and helping them get these needs met through their work.

- Use coaching to empower young professionals to move from new hire to peak performer.

- When giving feedback, be specific and timely, keep the focus on behaviors, make it the right kind of personal, and have a follow-up plan.

- Be as comfortable in the role of coachee as you are in the role of coach.

- Shift employee obstacles and mistakes into opportunities to learn and grow.

- Remind new hires about the grounds for assessment they have agreed to, and hold them accountable to your co-created vision of achievement.

- Carrots in moderation are okay. Just make sure that they are linked to a narrative that includes intrinsic motivators.

- If you and your company have invested in setting your young professional up to succeed and she hasn't, let her go at the end of 90 days.

chapter 7

Keep Their Focus on Their Focus

"I can be my own obstacle or I can be my own opportunity.
The difference is in how I choose to see."

Yours Truly

I recently received an email from a colleague telling me that Las Vegas "is *not* the place to be." I had asked her for an introduction at her old company, and she quickly shot me back an email communicating that she wished me well (questionable), was unable to help (or at least unwilling), and she couldn't wait until her child graduated school so that she could move out of our city. In the meantime, she wasn't going to be doing anything but "serving her time." As a little background, this is a person who told me when we first met that she hated her job and if only she could do [blank], then she would be overjoyed. Of course, the minute she got herself doing [blank], she found a new problem—Las Vegas. And I guarantee that if and when she moves, in less than a few months a new [blank] will emerge.

Have you ever noticed that some people, maybe even you, continue to experience one bad thing after another? Whether it's dysfunctional work or romantic relationships, a string of unfulfilling jobs or even a barrage of health crises, if you're anything like me you've spotted that some people seem to keep getting served heartache and misfortune. Yet if you stop and think about it, the same can also be said for those people who seem to always have a smile on their face. Who always get that promotion. Who always are thriving in their relationships. If we put our focus on something—good or bad—we tend to keep creating more of it.

This has tremendous implications on what you onboard your young professionals to see. Do you want them to see opportunities or do you want them to see obstacles? Do you want them to treat the symptoms of problems or look a little deeper to combat the sources? While every successful person I have ever met has her own special—and sometimes secret—recipe for how she achieved her heights, almost all of them mention the importance of focus. If you want young professionals to succeed, help them weed out distractions—in thoughts, beliefs, feelings, behaviors, and specific actions—and root themselves in ways of being and performing that shine a light on and reproduce what is right.

ZERO TOLERANCE FOR TRIANGULATION

Most young professionals are breathtaking gossips. Between infotainment shows like *TMZ* and *The Insider*, celebrity magazines such as *InTouch* and *Star*, and the advent of texting and tweeting, they have had equal opportunities to observe gossiping and refine their own practice of it.

> **Aa** **Triangulation**—by which I mean gossiping or outright complaining about people, procedures, roles, or anything else work-related to someone other than to whom the discontent is directed toward—is a cancer for any workplace. It's most treatable, like any cancer, when you engage in preventative care rather than allowing it to emerge and trying to treat it retroactively.

You and your company might define triangulation differently. What's important is that you know what it means to you and you communicate clearly to your new hires that it is self-defeating, unprofessional, and won't be tolerated. While you may do this during your formal onboarding program, make sure that you follow up on it a couple of months in at the time when employees are most likely starting to feel brazen enough to name what's bugging them. When young professionals take issue with something in your workplace, give them the permission to address it with the person who is the source. Remind them to utilize what they have learned about effective communication. If they feel uncomfortable going directly to the person, let them speak confidently with you, a mentor, or a trusted team member to rehearse the conversation confidentially. The key is that such a conversation be rooted in resolution and be a safe space to develop a strategy for how to move forward. To ensure that these conversations are genuinely results-oriented, request that a new hire set a day and time to have a face-to-face conversation with the person in question, report back to you when that is and share with you the outcome. (Note: in chapters 8 and 9 we will look at how to make other people right—without compromising our beliefs and feelings—and how to diffuse conflict when it arises.)

At times, triangulation arises when there is an inherent mismatch between an employee and a company. Irrespective of how keenly you recruit, interview, train, and onboard a new employee, it happens. What can't happen is ignoring it or treating the symptom rather than the source. If people are not happy and are unable or incapable of making the choice to be happy, let everyone move on by giving them permission to leave.

When RecycleBank's CEO Jonathan Hsu joined the company, he admits that inside the organization's four walls there was a fair amount of discontent. After making very clear his vision for the next stage of the groundbreaking environmental sustainability organization—creating a world where *nothing* is wasted—and sharing his strategy for addressing the hiccups that had emerged during the social enterprise's aggressive growth, he gave employees the opportunity to "exhibit the intellectual honestly to say this isn't for me." He helped 15 of the approximately 180 employees who felt that there was not complete alignment, energy, and enthusiasm to part ways. He even supported them to find their next opportunity. When you create a culture free of the typical and draining drizzle of persistent complaint, you keep employees focused on what can be rather than what isn't, and everyone is grateful for it.

ALWAYS HAVE A FILTER QUESTION

DAY 21

The guru of women's online business marketing, Marie Forleo, talks about the importance of always having a "filter question." It's easy to think that just because you have named what you or your young professionals are working toward in the short and long term, it is going to happen. Unfortunately, thinking and actualizing are interrelated but do not necessarily enjoy a cause and effect relationship.

 According to Marie, "a **filter question** is a simple question that you ask yourself that helps guide your actions and decisions on a daily basis." It supports you to put "your time and attention exactly on where you want to go the fastest." It helps you weed out behaviors, tasks, systems, and sometimes even goals that sound like opportunities but actually are obstacles toward what you are specifically seeking to achieve.

Help young professionals to identify the best filter question based on their roles, responsibilities, and career development plan. For example, let's imagine that you are the manager of an insurance agency. One of your new hires has the goal of closing a minimum of five clients per week. Without a filter question, the young professional is likely obsessing over how to get in as many weekly coffee appointments as possible, literally stalking every person she meets at her networking events until they agree to give her an hour of time. With the simple filter question, "How is this moving me toward my five closes?" she will hopefully realize that although she's working hard she isn't working so smart. She's likely wasting a lot of time going to events and chatting up people who either are perfectly happy with their existing insurance, do not have the means to invest in your insurance, or are simply expressing interest due to discomfort, but won't actually show up or even bother to cancel their appointment when the day comes.

With the filter question, the young professional realizes she should stop casting such a wide net. Instead, it's more strategic for her to focus on attending events and scheduling meetings with people who are clear they have a problem she—via your products—can fix.

She may even start doing informational presentations for her networking groups so that people who are genuinely curious about what she has to offer come right to her.

SAY YES BY SAYING NO

So what happens when the answer to one's filter question is a resounding no? *This thing I'm doing, this way I'm thinking, or this belief I'm holding onto is not serving me and needs to be filtered out.* Here is where a lot of young professionals feel like they're treading water—saying "uh-uh," "sorry," "no can do." While young professionals are often perceived as whiny, entitled, lazy, and so forth, the majority of them are veteran people-pleasers and will say "yes" and underperform before they harness the courage to say "no" with a logical and compelling explanation.

Break this habit! Teach your young professionals that in order to consistently say "yes" to their roles, responsibilities, goals, and so forth, they have to know when and how to be comfortable saying "no" in a variety of contexts. Saying "no" might mean creating and upholding boundaries between oneself and others. For example, turning down the opportunity to serve on a committee or spearhead a new project. Encourage young professionals to practice communicating their "no's" to you before delivering them to other team members so that you can help them build an appropriate response. Help them recognize the difference between butterflies in their stomach—that signal they are pushing outside their comfort zone and should press forward—from a gnawing misgiving that they're getting off course.

USE THE PAYOFF AS A CARROT

DAY 14

As discussed in the last chapter, carrots are okay when someone is doing mundane work. They can also be a reward for a one-off project or for work that just isn't going to ever light someone's fire. You can also use the payoff for accomplishing a goal or completing a project as a carrot for young employees. As you know, the current generation of young professionals loves to be lauded for their genuine accomplishments, and a sense of achievement is a far better engagement strategy than throwing money or a fancy title at them. It's cheaper, can be used repeatedly, and it works!

Enable young professionals to get clear on what it will look, feel, smell, sound, and taste like to accomplish individual, departmental, and organizational goals. How will this achievement affect their career development plan? Reflect on their professional portfolio? Position them for a promotion? Allow the department to stand out in the company? Take the company from start-up to public? As you help your young professionals paint the evocative picture, elicit their suggestions for how to celebrate the achievement and pivotal benchmarks along the way. While some will appreciate a simple and private acknowledgement, for others—as we saw in the example of Sodexo—a mention in a staff meeting or company newsletter will go a long way.

KEEP AN EYE ON THE TWO STEPS AHEAD

DAY 90

When young professionals see the payoff for achieving goals, it will be easier for them to focus on the long-term plan. (And note, while most generations think of long-term as five to 10 years down the line, young professionals think of long-term as one to two years.) As your new hires get ready to complete their orientation period with you, they have likely also completed a series of short-term tasks that comprised their chief responsibilities. In your conversations about how their first quarter unfolded and what lies ahead for the next quarter, frame their new or continuing responsibilities and achievement goals with what the next one to two years look like for them. Link this conversation—which should consistently be revisited now that your young professional has her footing—both to the role she is in as well as to the career trajectory she envisions for herself. When a young professional understands that what she is engaged in now is sowing the seeds for a particular outcome for the company and for herself, naturally she will be more focused and motivated to succeed.

I was fortunate to have a supervisor early on in my career who made what by any measure could have been seen as an exploitive experience ultimately an enjoyable one. As some background, in this internship my manager was paying me $6.00 an hour for which I was supposed to create a company newsletter, research and write grants, promote our programs to all of our constituents, and by the end of my first year with the organization, teach a series of classes on entrepreneurship. Of course I was in way over my head and came home most days shaking in my shoes. What my supervisor helped me to see after a few months was that this short-term work was direct preparation for me to reach my goal of becoming a nonprofit leader. If I wanted to run my own organization, I was going to need to know how to hustle for funding, and court clients and board members. I had the opportunity to get the kinks out then while I was young, so that by the time I had increasingly responsible leadership opportunities, I had already discovered my best practices. This simple shift in seeing the correlation between my day-to-day work and my long-term goal enabled me to show up for the remainder of my time eager to do my work. Now, please don't think I'm giving you license to overwork your young professionals.

Rather, my intention is to emphasize the importance of helping them see the relationship between what they're doing in the present and what they aspire to be doing in the future. There's not a doubt in my mind that I would not have founded and been running a nonprofit organization in college had I not had the experiences—the good, the bad, and the confusing—at the aforementioned company.

TIME LEADERSHIP TRUMPS TIME MANAGEMENT

DAY 14

Learning how to organize our time is instrumental to creating and sustaining integration between the various spheres of our lives. As a culture, we tend to think of time as something that we must put a harness around and control. But like people, time does not give us what we want simply because we force our will onto it. We need to replace the widespread tendency to work long and hard with working smart and gracefully. This begins with our relationship to time.

The most important shift to facilitate for young professionals is from thinking about time as something to control to thinking about it as something to work with. You can have employees make a list of 20 beliefs they have about time as a starting point into the conversation. For example: *There are always two to three fewer hours in a day than I need.* Or perhaps: *Time speeds up when I'm interested in what I'm doing and slows down when I couldn't care less.* Support young professionals to reframe misguided beliefs they have about time and, if appropriate, set new habits and goals that will enable them to see time as something that empowers rather than undermines them. Make sure that they are defining time in a way that supports high achievement and professional and personal well-being. For example: *Time is the 1,440 minutes each day where I shift possibilities into realities.*

A second strategy is to ask young professionals to create two different lists. In the first, have them make note of the range of activities they do over the course of a typical week, listing them in order from activities that they are best at and make them feel strong, through to the activities that deplete, bore, or challenge them. For the second list, ask them to list the days and hours of the workweek where they feel most alert and engaged through to the days and hours of the workweek that make them feel tired and disengaged. Then, encourage them to structure their week so that they are aligning their most important and enjoyable work with their peak times for performance. Partner with them to think through how they can shift their attitudes and beliefs around the times that are not playing to their strengths so that it's the former moments they replay in their heads. And as appropriate, sandwich the latter moments and activities between short breaks in the day to lessen their impact.

Third, encourage young professionals to create boundaries between themselves and their time and energy drains. Ask them to be clear on how they can stay engaged in important tasks regardless of inevitable distractions and communicate this to you and anybody else who may knowingly or unknowingly be undermining their time leadership. Be clear on your expectations for email, phone usage, and unscheduled meetings, ensuring that your philosophies and protocols truly support peak performance. A senior vice president of operations at an international nonprofit that I recently coached found an additional 15 hours in his workweek by checking email and responding to phone calls twice per day and limiting his daily meetings to a rotating two-hour block of time. While at first he scoffed at my challenge to create structures for his daily time allowance on communication, he came back to me elated when in less than two weeks he had created the first draft of a strategic plan he'd been unable to find the time to work on for the last 12 months!

TO DO OR TO DELEGATE...KNOW THE DIFFERENCE

DAY 60

As you hopefully know if you are responsible for other employees' success, knowing which of your assignments you should hold onto and which you should assign elsewhere is vital. More and more young professionals are in positions where either an intern or a more junior staff member reports to them. While your young professional may not be directly supervising them—and even if they are, alas, this is beyond the scope of the book—they need to be primed to strategically delegate their work.

If your young professional is a recovering serial overachiever—what I affectionately refer to as an RSO (and to be clear, I am one)—or has had negative group experiences and believes she needs to do everything important to ensure it gets done well, you may be combatting limiting beliefs such as "It will just be easier if I do it myself." Telling them to delegate because it's the right thing to do is rarely successful. Instead, enable young professionals to discover the benefits themselves. This can be as simple as asking them to observe you in practice. Choose two similar tasks that have multiple components to them. Have them shadow you as you complete one entirely on your own. Similarly, have them shadow you and anyone else to whom you delegate components of task two. Ask them to describe the differences in outcome—in terms of time, focus, energy, and so forth.

To set them up to delegate successfully, make sure they understand the following sequential steps to effective delegation. First, they must be very clear on what the final result will look like and work backward to identify all the steps that are necessary. Second, they should look over each of the steps and determine which people can complete each successfully with little to no guidance and supervision. Naturally, these are going to be at the top of the list to delegate. Next, they want to look for any pieces for which they are most qualified, excited by, or simply must complete. "Must" is tricky because it's so subjective. It usually encompasses anything that is confidential or very role-specific. These should stay with them. For anything that remains, help them to make the choice about what will better serve the efficient and effective completion of the goal. For everything that is in the to-delegate pile, they can now identify to whom it will go. Before soliciting their agreement, teach them to outline the deadline, step-by-step directions, and how they will follow up so that they communicate this clearly. Then, instruct young professionals to carry out their follow-up plan, make any adjustments that they determine are necessary—giving further directions, adjusting deadlines, or if necessary, taking back control over work—and enjoy the opportunity to focus on their narrower focus.

Even if a young professional has no one to delegate assignments to, knowing how to flex the delegation muscle will help them with their time leadership. For example, there may be minutia work they are doing that is never urgent and never important that they need to let go of. Similarly, understanding delegation will enable them to identify assignments they should not be taking on. It will help them make the necessary, compelling case when you or any other team member assigns them something they should not take on, so they can get back into focus and efficiency mode.

GET OUT OF YOUR OWN WAY BY GETTING OUT OF YOUR HEAD

Limiting beliefs certainly do not end with how young professionals think about time. The way young professionals think about themselves, their colleagues, their work, their clients, and your company has a tremendous impact on whether or not they stay focused on achieving results or on the never ending stream of possibilities for how they can fall short of them.

A **limiting belief** is any way of thinking that does not serve a person well, and therefore keeps her from her full potential for success and happiness.

There are a few limiting beliefs that young professionals particularly hold onto. They often are around the way they think about themselves. *I'm not smart enough. I'm not experienced enough. I don't communicate well enough.* Underlying a limiting belief about the self is almost always the message, I'm not _____ enough. While young professionals are purported to be egomaniacs who hold a deluded self-perception that they can do no wrong, the reality is that this so-called "puffing," as you may remember we explored a few chapters back, is often a poor attempt to compensate for low self-esteem.

When not thinking about their own performance, young professionals often spend a lot of time thinking about how others are thinking about them. One of my clients, who I'll call Holly, particularly exemplifies this. Holly is a quintessential young professional employee—she works hard and thinks even harder. It's not uncommon for Holly to put in 10–12 hour days at her PR firm because she is so committed to impressing the people she works with. When Holly does not receive a lot of feedback—which is pretty often given that she has had several managers who subscribe to their own outdated belief that feedback is primarily to correct mistakes—she starts thinking about what her leaders think of her. While Holly is lucky not to let this get in the way of her performance, all of this unnecessary worry and mental chatter definitely exhausts her and has played a role in her jumping departments every few months in hopes of getting more feedback, support, and coaching. And of course each time she makes a lateral leap, her company has to find her replacement.

Irrespective of what one's limiting beliefs are, as their name suggests, they limit possibilities, creativity, resiliency, enthusiasm—and most of all, they limit focus. Introduce the question, "How is that thought affecting your success?" to your young professionals as early as possible. Encourage them to ask it of themselves *any* time they notice a shift in their thinking from possibility to problem. If the answer is that the thought they are creating shines a light on obstacles instead of opportunities, instruct them to reframe it. You can even poke fun at the notion that they are "entitled" to their beliefs—"Sure, Josh, you are entitled to get frustrated when somebody interrupts you while you're speaking. But as Dr. Phil asks, 'How's that working out for you?'" No matter how old we are, when we can recognize that a way of thinking we're clinging to isn't helping us to do our best work or play our biggest game, we can usually pretty quickly self-correct. And for young professionals who are in their first 90 days and starting to solidify workplace habits, this soft skill is perhaps one of the most important to develop.

ENCOURAGE A PRAXIS APPROACH

One of the best ways to enable young professionals to get out of their heads is to help them adopt a praxis approach.

Praxis, according to the renowned Brazilian educational philosopher Paulo Freire, is taking action, reflecting upon it, and taking new informed action—which leads to transformation. Rather than suffering from idea inebriation—where you sit and muse until you have eye strain and a migraine—when you practice the art of praxis you recognize that sometimes done is better than perfect.

Support young professionals to see that it takes a lot of trial and a fair amount of error to do their best work. Keep them focused on results and the necessary action required to achieve them by helping them view the hiccups to success they encounter—both the foreseen and the unanticipated—as opportunities that will help them "transform," as Freire would say, when they take action the next time around.

For Cher Hale, adopting a praxis approach to her work as social media director for Hero School—a social enterprise that provides character development education for marginalized communities—has enabled her to stay focused on building Hero School's visibility by having the freedom to try new things. The benchmark for success: Do her ideas drive the business bottom line? When Cher began at Hero School, she was focused primarily on building the organization's online profile by engaging with current and prospective volunteers, funders, and other fans through Facebook and Twitter. She soon realized that while social media was useful in connecting with some of the Hero School community, she was not getting as much engagement as she or Hero School's executive director hoped for. So Cher suggested writing a twice-a-month newsletter. While Hero School's tribe might not be lighting it up on social media, Cher suspected they were reading their emails.

Even though Cher knew she had a lot to learn, she wasted no time drafting the basic format and an inaugural edition for the e-newsletter. Rather than worrying about getting it perfect, she got it done. In two weeks she was ready to show it to her supervisor. "The first time," Cher admits, "he changed about 50 percent of the copy. But by the second time, he only changed about 25 percent." Cher was learning quickly. And the more she was able to reflect upon her work and apply her learning to future editions, the more freedom her boss gave her. "My boss began to let me experiment with various fonts, story ideas, pictures, and headings. After each newsletter, I would take a look at the analytics from a day after to a week after." Cher's conversion rate for people opting in after reading the newsletter was initially just over 20 percent. As she continued to tweak her work to capitalize on what her audience was clicking on, she was able to boost conversions to 30 percent. By applying a praxis approach, Cher improved the aesthetics and content of her newsletter and achieved the goal of increasing community engagement.

ASSIGN "VICE" WORK

DAY 30 Most managers have a lot of choices about how to assign work. Nevertheless, it's so easy to give it little thought and make a unilateral decision to do it either according to title, length of time at a company, assumptions about who likes what, and so forth. The more your young professionals like what they are doing, the more they can stay focused on it. Use what you know about your employees' particularly motivators, their career plans, and so forth, as well as what they tell you is most engaging, to determine short- and long-term tasks that are "vice" for them.

In case you're wondering, I picked up the concept of "vice" work from pioneering theatre director Anne Bogart. Back in my performer days, I had the opportunity to make original theatre with Anne and her theatre company, SITI. One of the challenges of devising creative work from scratch is knowing what belongs in the world you are trying to create. A world in a theatre piece should be as clear as the world from the quintessential 1980s TV show *Miami Vice*. Anne encouraged performers to try out a lot of different possibilities—with respect to images, stories, text—but ultimately we all had to do a "vice" test on it. If the idea didn't create as clear of a world as *Miami Vice*, we had to strike it.

While in your initial first months it might take a bit of experimentation to identify what is "vice" for your young professional, ultimately you want to give them as many opportunities to play in this sweet spot as possible. Determining "vice" can be a group process. At Nourish International, a team of young managers actually elicited the input of their interns to see what management practices were working the best for the group. What emerged both from the interns' responses and honest conversations with the young executive director (ED) was that the ED found managing the interns a chore—something he didn't have the time and energy to invest in. Without enough leadership, his interns' performance suffered. On the flip side, the COO loved working directly with the interns. And it showed. Her team felt well-trained, well-supported, appropriately challenged, and raved about their experience with the company. Leaving ego at the door, both the ED and COO realized the latter should be the one doing the direct managing, training, establishing workload, and giving feedback, while the ED would focus on more of the organizational leadership and retain direct access to the interns for the projects where it was appropriate.

As the Ancient Greek playwright Sophocles said, "Look and you will find it." Help your young professionals develop the gaze of professional success. Develop their ability to cast the gaze equally on the results they seek and the beliefs, thoughts, feelings, and actions that enable the desired outcome. Let time be everyone's friend. Filter out everything that gets in the way. Ensure that you call out and squelch the distractor of gossip. And above all else, let everything your young professionals do be motivated from a sense of opportunity rather than obstacle.

Tweet-Sized Takeaways

- Zap gossip before it ever begins. Because once it does, it will be cancerous to your new hire and everyone else.

- Weed out unnecessary thoughts, feelings, and behaviors by having a filter question.

- When young professionals answer their filter questions with a "no," ensure that they translate that "no" into action.

- Keep young professionals focused by directing their attention to the sense of achievement that comes from meeting goals.

- A young professional who can connect present actions to future outcomes can more easily sustain focus.

- When young professionals have a healthy concept of time, they set themselves up to use it efficiently.

- Teach young professionals how to decide when to delegate and how to do it effectively.

- Ensure that young professionals zap limiting beliefs—particularly any that encourage them to think of obstacles instead of opportunities.

- If you want young professionals to quickly get into action, encourage them to apply a praxis approach.

- Finally, to avoid letting them get distracted, let young professionals play to their interests and enthusiasm.

chapter 8

Develop Impeccable Customer Service Skills

"Service, in short, is not what you do, but who you are.
It is a way of living that you need to bring to everything you
do, if you are to bring it to your customer interactions."

Betsy Sanders

As consumers, your young professionals care about their customer service more than any previous generation. They patronize companies like Apple and Zappos as much for the experience they will have—one-on-one customer support or free expedited shipping—as they do for the product. Young professionals have also been consumers longer than any previous generation. Companies have marketed directly to them since they were in diapers, and many young professionals had buying power in their homes via their allowance or a credit card before they had any form of employment. It's not unusual for your young professional to take to social media to spread the word about a terrific customer service experience—or one that was disappointing or downright unacceptable. They understand that as consumers their customer feedback has power. After one of my worst customer service experiences, I attempted to call the company and was transferred haphazardly from one extension to the next until I finally decided to hang up and send a 135-character tweet about the ageism, racism, and overall rudeness I had experienced. As a result, I had a call from a senior VP at corporate within 48 hours!

Because customer service is a muscle that needs to be flexed, however, young professionals' experiences as engaged consumers do not automatically translate into keen skills and behaviors as providers. More and more companies are putting all of their young professionals through a customer service onboarding experience—not just those who formally perform the function—in order to combat the range of common deficits, for example: inappropriate dress, disinterest in customers, or inability to problem solve. Whether you have a formal customer service onboarding program or not, employing the following tactics will set young professionals up to be customer and colleague-centered in their work.

FRAME CUSTOMER SERVICE AS A FORM OF NETWORKING

Your young professionals are the most entrepreneurial generation in American history. Not only do approximately 50 percent of them perceive self-employment as more secure than a full-time job, but approximately 80 percent hope at some point to own a business. Young professionals know that the key to launching any new idea or business venture is building a tribe of interested people. Therefore, whether their roles are directly linked to customer service or not, talking about customer service as a necessary muscle to flex for their own professional relationship-building and career trajectory is much more likely to make an impact than simply telling them it's important to you or your company.

> **Aa** Enable young professionals to see **customer service** as the ongoing art and practice of providing value to co-workers, managers, and colleagues, as well as to customers and clients.

When you enable young professionals to shift from thinking of customer service as a task performed by a low-level employee, they will want to do it well. They will see its impact on their current and future success. They will invest the time and energy necessary for mastery. And because the cornerstone of effective networking is building mutually beneficial relationships, teach young professionals how to recognize and respond to others' needs. Encourage them to keep their eyes open for people who are overwhelmed and, if appropriate, reach out and see how they can alleviate their stress. Many of my strongest professional relationships were built from seeing someone with a great idea and asking how I could be of service. Even if there's nothing your young professional can "do," help her recognize that there is value simply in the asking.

LISTEN FOR WHAT IS BEING SAID

DAY 14

In his book *Quiet Leadership*, author David Rock identifies 10 reasons people don't hear what another person is saying—whether they are giving a formal, hour-long presentation or simply sharing an idea casually in a conversation. They include:

- listening for opportunities to sound intelligent

- listening for a chance to seem funny

- listening for how you can sound important

- listening to get information you want

- listening to external distractions such as other noises, music, and so forth

- listening for what's going on with the other person

- listening for your own thoughts, and not listening at all

- listening to see how you can help

- listening to understand the problem

- listening for how you can benefit.

While Rock is not writing specifically about generational listening blocks, as you look at the list, I'm sure you are identifying that many of these are showing up for your young professionals even in their first couple of weeks of work. A simple way to draw their attention to them is to first ask them to recap what they heard being said after a short conversation. Second, ask them what went through their heads as they were listening in the conversation. Most likely you will discover that more time was spent thinking about their own thinking—either in analyzing the message or formulating their next thought—than being really planted in the here and now.

Rather than spending too much time diagnosing and then telling your young professionals to weed out their distractions, encourage them to follow Rock's suggestion and "listen for potential." To listen for potential, a young professional is directing her focus to a speaker's line of thinking and toward what she wants. This is particularly useful in a customer service context. As Rock says, "By choosing to listen to people as successful, competent, and able to resolve their own dilemmas, guess what's likely to happen? They often solve their own problems." For your young professional, listening for potential—for what the person speaking desires—means they will "find themselves being very present and in the moment, and, above all, having a much better time as they listen." Take caution when doing this work with young professionals that you keep the focus on the positive and the active. For if you reinforce what they *shouldn't* do, they will unfortunately just do more of it—in this case, create more distractions for themselves.

LISTEN FOR WHAT IS *NOT* BEING SAID

It's one thing for young professionals to listen more adeptly. Yet the best listening often comes from recognizing what the person speaking is not directly saying. For young professionals to sustain a service orientation with customers, colleagues, and anyone else in their professional life, they must know how to read and respond to nonverbal cues. Given that young professionals frequently communicate virtually, they are not practiced at interpreting facial expressions, hand gestures, eye contact, posturing, proximity to others, and the many meanings of silence.

I once worked with a manager who made the most egregious facial grimaces any time she disapproved of a choice a staff member was making. Which was often. Now as you know, I'm an older member of Generation Y, yet it was painfully clear to me when this manager was forming mental judgments in her head. This was not so clear, however, to her younger Gen Y staff. In fact, they would often report how surprised they were in weekly feedback sessions when this manager would express disappointment in choices they had made. They felt it was coming out of left field. If they didn't hear it, it simply wasn't being said.

By simply addressing that communication not only encompasses words, but everything done with the body, you empower your young professionals to observe these facets of communication in others and in themselves. If you do not have the opportunity to put young professionals in communication training that lets them develop their nonverbal communication competency, you can point out nonverbal communication by replaying conversations you have with them. First, let a conversation unfold naturally. Then, you can replay it either at a much greater distance, much closer together, without eye contact, with a lot of eye contact, with one person sitting and the other standing, and so forth. Afterward, debrief with young professionals what they observed about how the conversational dynamics changed. Challenge them to apply these observations in their communication with others—both to read the cues others are presenting and, just as importantly, to make adjustments in their own nonverbals to drive communication exchanges toward the results they seek.

ASK QUESTIONS FROM A PLACE OF CURIOSITY

DAY 14

In their customer service training for new bank tellers, Nevada State Bank prepares young professionals to make small talk. They teach new hires to read clues from their customers, for example: a picture of a child on one's key chain, or a button on a handbag promoting a social cause, as conversation starters. Most importantly, they teach young professionals to push through fear that they are overstepping boundaries and ask personal questions of their customers. As Maria Gutierrez, VP training supervisor explains, "You need to know a customer's needs in order to deliver on them. When you ask the right questions, you know how to give a customer the experience *they* want."

Whether you are giving your young professionals the permission to ask questions such as: "Tell me what's most important to you in _____?" or "For you to become a raving fan of our company, what would need to happen?," you want young professionals to be genuinely curious in their interactions with customers, colleagues, and anyone else they encounter. Whether I'm teaching people how to coach or simply be more present in their interpersonal communication, I recommend following five basic principles to asking good questions. First, ask questions that are open-ended. "How has our leisure guide enhanced your travel experience?" yields much more useful information than "Has our leisure guide enhanced your travel experience?"

The second and third principles are directly related. Ask one question at a time. Let the person you are speaking with have time to answer fully. Help young professionals resist the temptation to jump in and ask follow-up questions. In their desire to help the people they are speaking with, oftentimes they inadvertently stack questions and actually make it more difficult for a person to answer. "Tell me Daniel, do you like our service? And if so, would you say that you like the fact that we have extended hours now on weekends? Or is that something you haven't taken advantage of? But if you were to take advantage, would that be a helpful feature for you or not make much of an impact?" It's much easier to ask

Daniel, "What is the top benefit you've received from our service?" A young professional can always ask another question such as, "How important are extended weekend hours to you?" If Daniel should hem and haw, most likely his silence means he's just thinking. Teach young professionals, many of whom may not understand that silence can be a good thing, to imagine they have their hands over their mouths, smile, be present, and wait for an answer.

Fourth, just as you want young professionals to listen for possibility, you want them to ask questions that open up possibilities. It's easy for young professionals to interpret this as asking questions about what they or their companies can do better. This is a part of that principle. You can help young professionals go one step further in the possibility generation by asking questions that help someone imagine their desired outcome. It's a way to honor that someone has a problem without reinforcing the problem and keeping that person on the hamster wheel. For example, "If you were able to have more time in your day, what would you do with it?" would be a terrific way for a young professional hawking personal organization software to help a prospective client get sold on the outcome. While people make the majority of their purchasing (and hiring decisions) to solve problems, it's most compelling when they see themselves on the other side of the problem.

Finally, ask questions only when you are not attached to the answer. This can be tricky, particularly for young professionals who have that desire to be right. They want to be lauded for their work. Support them to see that if they are leading someone with a question such as, "Now tell me, who has provided the best service experience for you at Fiona's Fabric House?" then it's best not to ask. Naturally, the person being asked will know that the person asking is phishing for her own name, so the customer won't give a truthful answer, and she will feel like she needs to take a shower after the exchange to wash her dirty feeling off.

MIRROR BACK WHAT YOU OBSERVE

Just as the name suggests, **mirroring** is the art of reflecting back to a person what we are picking up from them.

For young professionals, mirroring is one of the simplest and most effective ways to convey an interpersonal wisdom beyond their years. It enables them to connect with whomever they are speaking and reinforce or adjust any perceptions they have about where someone is coming from. The most common way for young professionals to mirror is through their language. For example, you might be communicating to your young professional her top three action items for the next week. While it's easy to think that your young professional heard, "I need you to compile a list of all the funders who have not continued their funding this grant cycle," it's possible that your young professional instead heard, "compile a list of funders who are continuing their funding this grant cycle." This mistake could occur either because she wasn't present and fully listening, or was listening too hard and therefore missed the important word, "not." When you get young professionals in the habit of saying as a way to check in, "So what I'm hearing you say is—" you empower them to follow through on what the person they are speaking with expects. You also strengthen their ability to be present and listen for possibility.

You can also develop young professionals' ability to mirror nonverbal body language—

such as eye contact, gestures, and posture. Establish that mirroring is not about mimicking a person. Intention and subtlety are key here. The aim is to facilitate connection rather than one up someone or exacerbate a tense exchange. Teach young professionals to sustain the level of eye contact that the people they are speaking with desire. While I think eye contact is genuinely a good thing for young professionals as American audiences read it as confident and competent communication, it's most important for young professionals to give the amount the person they are speaking with is giving them.

Young professionals can also use mirroring in their nonverbal communication physically. When a young professional can tell that someone is pulling a power play and chooses to stand up and take up space to make herself unable to be dismissed, it's a beautiful thing. Similarly, I am blown away when young professionals are so connected to the people they are speaking with that they match their breathing to that other person. One of the easiest nonverbal cues you can train your young professionals to mirror is facial expression, particularly in traditional customer service. If and when a client is enthusiastic about a product or service and is grinning ear-to-ear, there is often no greater way of closing the sale than for a young professional simply to mirror that smile back.

MAKE PEOPLE FEEL VALIDATED

DAY 21

When young professionals use mirroring, one of the benefits is that the person they are speaking to feels validated. And let's face it, most of us have an inherent desire to be truly seen and heard by others. We want people to respect our opinions. We want people to view us as competent in our work and to take action based on what we say. Nevertheless, we don't always give people the gift of our attention and validation.

And typically the less power we feel we have in a situation, the more pronounced our desire becomes to be right, aggressive, and powerful. You see it in employees who seem to take on sickening amounts of glee telling people to wait in one-to-two hour long lines. Or in telephone customer service reps who keep repeating the amount you were charged rather than explaining why you were charged the amount. It's as if they were onboarded for the sole purpose of driving their customers batty. Unfortunately, if you orient young professionals to their roles with little to no consideration for how their behavior makes your customers feel, they will perform the same way. They've undoubtedly experienced it hundreds of times themselves. And as the expression goes, "monkey see, monkey do."

Irrespective of what your young professionals can or can't do to design a top-notch experience for the people they interface with—and again, this is as important a principle for designing mutually beneficial interoffice relationships as it is for designing client service—they *can* communicate in a way that makes people feel validated. At one Las Vegas casino, the director of training enables new hires, the majority of whom are young professionals, to experience firsthand the frustration that many guests have felt when they are not validated. In his customer service training, the director takes real feedback from TripAdvisor, the number one online site for hospitality reviews, and lists them on PowerPoint slides as Twitter messages from hypothetical past guests. While young professionals might laugh to see "@BozoTheClown" say "Waited in line over an hour at the hotel coffee shop. Worst customer service ever" or "@MargeSimpson" comment "Checked in an hour late and the hotel didn't have my room ready. Lame," the exercise uses young professionals' affinity for social media brilliantly. It shows how one person's experience can go viral within seconds. And it helps a young professional step into the shoes of real past guests to see how they felt as a result of the service they experienced.

The director also enables young professionals to see the payoff for great customer service by asking new hires to recall their own positive experiences as customers at the hotel. After recounting the positive experience, the director pushes young professionals to see the role specific employees played in bringing that experience to life. In each of the examples the director shared with me, the underlying role was ensuring a customer felt validated, heard, and trusted—even in some of the more frustrating employee moments.

For example, one of the director's recent new hires remembered misplacing her ticket to the hotel's show when she left the theatre to use the bathroom. While an usher's first response would normally be, "I'm sorry, I can't let you back into the theater without your ticket," meaning the person would have to retrace her steps to the bathroom, possibly rummage through trash, and most likely go to a different usher to try to plead her case—missing a good chunk of the show—this usher began the conversation by explaining that he knew this must be a frustrating experience and not to worry. He asked the ticketholder where she was sitting and the names of the people in her party. The usher outside the theater was able to quickly radio to an usher inside to double-check the woman's story. The woman was in her seat immediately after. As evidenced by her recalling this experience at her new hire training, it clearly left a positive and lasting impact on her.

It's not difficult for a young professional to make a customer feel right. Most of the time it requires getting out of her way and meeting anger or frustration with kindness and empathy. In the following example, observe how retail customer service representative Rick will say very little to shopper Shoshanna when she comes in to return her netbook. But what he does say—both through the questions he asks and the suggestions he makes—communicates that he cares about where Shoshanna is coming from. See how he diffuses her anger, demonstrates that he trusts what she says, and brings closure to the situation by validating Shoshanna each step of the way.

Retailer Rick Plays Nice With Shopper Shoshanna

Rick: Hi, my name is Rick. How can I help you today?

Shoshanna: I want to return this piece of trash. It's not what I expected.

Rick: I'm sorry the netbook didn't work out for you. What about it didn't live up to your expectations?

Shoshanna: It just doesn't work for me.

Rick: I see that you have a receipt so I can take care of this for you. I was just wondering if it was an operational problem or—

Shoshanna: Wait, you can take it back? Just like that? Oh, that's amazing. See, I got it so I wouldn't have to lug my laptop with me on the road, but it turns out that I'm not able to run my company's data management software on it. I'm pissed off because the guy who helped me pick it out said it would work. I didn't find out he was wrong until after I thought I had it all loaded, several thousand feet in the air. It really put me in a jam for a couple of weeks. I couldn't access any of the information I needed.

Rick: I'm very sorry that you were misguided and that meant you didn't have what you needed on your trip. I'll credit your account with the full amount right away.

Shoshanna: Wow, that was a lot easier than I thought. Thanks. I'm feeling a lot less ticked off now.

LET EVERYONE GET WHAT THEY NEED

As you see in the role play between Rick and Shoshanna, one of the easiest ways to diffuse conflict is to make the other person right. This is a key component of any negotiation.

> **Aa** For your purposes onboarding young professionals, I suggest you introduce **negotiation** as the process of getting multiple people's needs met. (Note: I'm using needs intentionally.) While people might want a lot of things, if people can get their needs met, they will most likely walk away happy and committed to the agreement.

When young professionals think about their call to action for a negotiation, they should link it to what each party needs. Let's imagine for a moment that Rick's company did not have a clear-cut return policy for items that worked. It would be easy for Rick to say to himself, "I need Shoshanna to keep her netbook so that I don't get into trouble for requesting a return on a non-defective item. I'm going to explain since it's not broken there's nothing I can do." A lot of young professionals show up to negotiations with this kind of mindset because that's how they've been trained to think. While it's not inherently bad to onboard young professionals to think in terms of profit and loss, if they don't think about other parties' needs, young professionals may actually be increasing loss. The customer doesn't come back. And not only does the customer not return, she stops future customers from purchasing—both existing and potential ones—by complaining about her negative experience. If a young professional is focused solely on her own needs, and develops a negotiation strategy based on a call to action that is all about her, she may get what she wants in the short-term, but not what is best for the company in the long-term.

Imagining again that Rick doesn't have free rein to do product returns, let's hope Rick's boss has read at least part of *90 Days, 90 Ways*, so Rick knows his primary need is to make Shoshanna a raving fan of the company in the most cost-effective way as possible. Rick wants her to share her positive experience with 100 of her closest friends, family members, and colleagues. Therefore, Rick gets to work identifying Shoshanna's needs as quickly as possible. He says much of what he said in the role play while incorporating more of the earlier tactics in the chapter. He listens for possibility and for what is not being said. Therefore, he asks open-ended questions like, "What is most frustrating for you right now?" and mirrors back what he is gathering.

If Shoshanna's need is to get money back in her pocket, the only way to meet it might be gaining permission to issue the refund. If this is the bottom-line, hopefully Rick is able to do that. It's quite possible based on how Rick has structured his conversation, however, that Shoshanna just wants her disappointment and frustration to be heard. Or perhaps she is still craving efficiency and mobility so there actually lies an opportunity for Rick to sell her a device that lets her run the software she desires on her netbook. Prime young professionals to facilitate negotiation conversations so that they get their own and other party's needs identified prior to proposing solutions. Understanding that in many negotiations—between governments, companies, colleagues, or significant others—what the parties involved most need is to feel heard or to be able to go back to their respective parties being able to report a "win," sets young professionals up to be successful.

SHOW THEM HOW TO "HOLD THE BEACH BALL"

DAY 30

In her go-to book for young professionals, *They Don't Teach Corporate in College*, business and workplace expert Alexandra Levit explains to her reader that it's not okay to "bounce" a question or request over to another colleague when you don't have an answer. The classic example of this, Alexandra points out, is the email forward function. "Please take a look at Charlie's question. Thanks, A." Not a great habit to forge, particularly once an employee has her feet wet and knows who and where to look for an answer. It is a nuisance for the person who has to catch the beach ball. And it's definitely a nuisance for the person wanting information who now has another person to chase down for it.

Being responsible for providing the information people seek comes back to the first tactic in the chapter, relationship building. For a relationship to thrive, you have to put some work into it. While some inquiries will truly be outside of an employee's purview and appropriate for her to delegate, most will be well within the realm of her role. Empower young professionals to "hold on to the beach ball" by showing them the payoff for doing so. As Alexandra says, it's important for young professionals not to "underestimate the importance of being the one who actually offers assistance and shepherds the issue through to a satisfying resolution." When a customer or co-worker sings your praises and word gets back to your company or manager that you took the time to go above and beyond to over deliver, that's a whole lot better than receiving a trophy. Ensure your young professionals know that when they provide value, prove themselves as genuine team players, and create enjoyable experiences for others, the payoff is vast and usually starts a chain reaction of positive results.

I can attest to the positive impact firsthand. Prior to launching my own company, one facet of my full-time job was administering a graduate education program. I was hungry to be in a different role—one that let me be the one educating—so I chose to use the days when I was parked at a desk to be useful to the people who called. I not only made a point of asking questions such as, "Tell me, what is it that is most attracting you to our program?" and "Is there anything else I can answer to help you decide—once and for all—if this is the right program for you?" I also made sure I got them answers to any of their questions. And there were some whoppers!

Being truly present each and every time I picked up that phone played out in dividends in my career trajectory. Actually, it's still paying. Because I showed up so fully to those phone conversations, I made some good friends, was asked to present at a prestigious conference, and have had employees and clients who I met via one of those phone conversations.

GIVE AUTHORITY TO MAKE LOW-LEVEL DECISIONS

DAY 30

In order for young professionals to truly hold on to the beach ball, they need to be able to make split second decisions. Ensure they know when they can make such calls. It's easy for companies to think that they are protecting themselves by having young talent always double check decisions—including those to honor customer requests—with a supervisor. In reality, though, this kind of micromanagement wastes customers' time and can make them unnecessarily ornery. It kills that young person's critical thinking abilities; they create the habit of never being able to trust their ideas and instincts. Most problematically, it slows down their ability to complete tasks and produce results.

Enterprise Rent-A-Car is just one of many companies that empower their customer service representatives, who are mostly young professionals, to solve a customer complaint themselves. If a customer reports that her car was not thoroughly cleaned or that she waited in line longer than expected, a representative is encouraged to ask, "How can I make the inconvenience up to you?" When the customer typically suggests, "Credit me a day on my rental" or "Next time I'd like a free upgrade," that young professional gets to be the good gal and say, "No problem." It should come as no surprise that at least in part due to role autonomy, Enterprise is incredibly popular with young professionals—yearly they hire between 7,000-8,000 new grads—and close to 100 percent of their senior management began as manager trainees with the company.

Follow Enterprise's lead. Give your young professionals the ability to honor inexpensive customer requests. To ensure they are not abusing privileges, track what they are offering customers. If anything appears fishy, address it immediately. This will send the signal that it is about serving customers, not extending favors. If you're feeling trepidatious, remember that each time you lose $50 or so by honoring a request, you are most likely developing a proselytizer who will bring new customers your way. Irk a customer, that person—particularly if young—will take it online and in 140 characters or less, drive current and prospective customers away from you.

ADMINISTER TRIAL RUNS

DAY 7

I think I can comfortably say you don't expect new employees to show up to work on day one and automatically know how to perform all facets of their job. Yet if your company is like most, you probably put them through some kind of formal or informal role training for a day or two and then expect them to be fully "on." And most likely for the first few days employees will be "on," at least when you're looking. They will be conscious incompetent—aware that they have to put a lot of attention toward their moment-to-moment tasks to perform them successfully. For young professionals, being in the conscious incompetent space is exhausting—so much so that when their direct supervisors aren't observing, oftentimes they let performance dip pretty dramatically in order to have the energy to be "on" again once supervisors reappear. For most employees, after "good" customer service has become habit (which as we know takes about 90 days) they will be in the unconscious competent space. They won't have to think about how to get it right for their customers. But how do you—and they—get there?

Let's explore how to solve the two key prongs of the problem: young new hires not being ready for customers, and being unprofessional when more senior staff are not around. First, as you may recall from chapter 5, young professionals often come to you as awkward face-to-face communicators. It's important for them to rehearse out loud exactly what you want them to say to customers. Don't assume they know how to greet, move a conversation along to a sale, or plant the seed for future patronage just because you have educated them on the features and benefits of your product or service. While you can create a script for customer interactions that makes room for a young professional's personality, make sure you are clear on what verbiage should always appear as well as any content that should not. Then, role play with your young professional for the variety of conversations they can expect, so that they can really get comfortable both with the content and with adapting to a living and breathing human being. Follow the strategies for effective feedback presented in chapter 6, and provide feedback in all the areas you care about, for example, the young professional's greeting, pitch, small talk, tone, and so forth. It's best if they have the opportunity to role play as a customer as well. Not only will it be a hoot for them to get to perform the "difficult" characters they inevitably come into context with, it also gives them an opportunity to see more experienced staff respond to these situations with grace and decorum.

Now, let's look at how to guard against young professionals performing great customer service only when they believe they are being observed. I recently spoke with a regional manager for a health diagnostic testing center who was shocked by the amount of complaints she had received about a new employee. While she admitted that the employee was on a performance improvement plan to clean up her rude customer communication, she said that each time she went into the center to observe the employee, the employee was doing everything right. Unfortunately, this well-intentioned manager didn't realize that the problem wasn't that the employee didn't know what to do. Initially, this might have been the case. However, even though she was observing "good" performance, by receiving the same negative customer feedback 60 days into the performance improvement plan, the problem was not a lack of training. While I'm not a fan of Big Brother tactics, when employees know they might have "secret shoppers"—or in the case of the health care diagnostic center, a "secret patient"—they are more likely to perform their work as the professionals you want them to be.

Every one of your young professionals is engaged in some form of customer service. As the adage goes, "customer service is not a department; it's everyone's job." While it's true that many young professionals are the primary people your clients interact with—they pick up phones, process orders, and handle exchanges and complaints—it's equally important to develop young professionals' customer service skills even if they are housed in a department that on the surface appears to have little to no bearing on your customer. For when your young professionals consistently show up to their work looking and behaving like professionals, build mutually beneficial relationships, over deliver on others' expectations, and diffuse conflict if and when it arises, they are going to enjoy their jobs more. As a result, they will deliver their work at a higher level of excellence and require less oversight from you.

Tweet-Sized Takeaways

- Tap young professionals' affinity for entrepreneurship and frame customer service as vital to building their network.

- Help young professionals be present in conversations by "listening for potential."

- Teach young professionals the key components of nonverbal communication and how to apply them in their communication.

- Train young professionals to follow the five principles of asking good questions.

- Mirror back language and physical communication to connect with people.

- Diffuse potential conflict by validating where people are coming from.

- Develop young professionals who negotiate to get each party's needs met.

- Show young professionals that when they "hold the beach ball," they are enhancing their value as an employee.

- Give young professionals the ability to make decisions on the spot.

- To make good customer service a habit, role play with young professionals and employ "secret" customers.

chapter 9

Grow Employees Who Create Company Calm

"Until we enter boldly into the fears we most want
to avoid, those fears will dominate our lives. But when
we walk directly into them—protected by the warm garb
of friendship or inner discipline or spiritual guidance—
we can learn what they have to teach us."

Parker Palmer

Most young professionals have been raised under the erroneous message that fear is the norm, yet it's to be avoided at all costs. Through their lives young professionals have seen fear repeatedly used as a catalyst for them to take action. Whether it's been to get vaccinated, earn good grades, vote a particular way, accrue debt or even pay off debt, the message has been "do this" and you'll get over the fear. Unfortunately, fear rarely abates. Nor should it be avoided. Fear is a normal physiological response our bodies produce. The reasons that fear arises and what that fear signals can change quite a bit, however.

In your pursuit of developing a new generation of effective, pleasant, and resilient employees, please shift the conversation around fear as early as possible. You empower young professionals to feel good in their heads and in their bodies when they recognize that while fear can signal impending danger, more often than not it's signaling they're on the cusp of something great—a novel idea or a big breakthrough in their performance. The key is learning how to demystify what the fear is about, make nice with it, and use it to move forward rather than to retreat.

Fear—like confidence, self-image, self-talk, happiness, and gratitude—is bandied around almost ad nauseam in the self-improvement world. These words need as much if not more face-time in the worlds of HR, management, and learning and development than the jargon we typically direct our attention to. For until professionals of any age learn how to foster healthy relationships with their own thoughts, feelings, and beliefs, good luck trying to engender sustainable peak performance from them. Debbie Kent, the director of human resources and organizational development for the Las Vegas Convention and Visitors Authority (LVCVA) agrees. "From an employee's very first day, we try to create an attitude of gratitude. We talk about how to be of service to others and wake up in the morning hitting the ground with the right foot. We even remind employees that in times of conflict they should remember that each person they encounter has come into their life for a reason. We hire 50 percent on background and 50 percent on attitude, so once an employee gets in the door we do what we can not to let them hit the snooze button and coast through their work." In the following tactics, we will explore how to develop the success-inducing habits, mindset, and behavior that the LVCVA engenders in your own young professionals to start a chain reaction of positive and calming effects for everyone in your company.

CREATE EMPLOYEES WITH A POSSIBILITY-CENTERED MINDSET

The best time to begin engendering healthy habits in thinking is on a young professional's first day, when she is often at her most nervous and self-critical. In chapter 2 we looked at a myriad of ways to allay new hire worries. This is a great starting point into helping young professionals habitually see opportunities instead of obstacles. Like any habit, though, it takes daily, intentional practice to show up to each day of work and to each conversation or decision seeing what can be rather than what cannot.

In pursuit of conditioning young professionals to see themselves, their colleagues, and their work consistently from a possibility-centered mindset, first and foremost you need to model this in your own thinking and behavior for your employees. Hopefully this goes without saying. One has no right asking a young professional, "Where's the treasure within this trash?" while going off about how stressed out you are or how unreasonable another one of your colleagues is. In addition to walking your talk and using the aforementioned question, you can use others such as "Where is the opportunity within this obstacle?" or "How can you receive this as a gift rather than as garbage?" to redirect a young professional from the negative to the positive. If you begin these practices day one with young professionals, you will notice that this way of thinking really becomes automatic by the end of the onboarding period, even if your young professional has had a history and habit of negative thinking.

 ## ENCOURAGE PEOPLE TO FEEL WHAT THEY'RE FEELING... FOR 90 SECONDS

One of the chief reasons why you want young professionals to exercise nutritious thinking is because thoughts fuel the way people feel. And because feelings motivate the actions we take, if you want young professionals achieving results, they need to be feeling good to make the best choices in their behaviors that will—or will not—get them to where you both want them to go. There is only one way people can affect the way they feel. It's by changing their thoughts—prior to allowing emotions to be engaged and immediately after.

There are a lot of conflicting views on how people, particularly young professionals and women, should express their feelings in the workplace. It's not my place to tell you how to tell other people to process their emotions. And because I have yet to see anyone in the workplace be successful at controlling her own or another's emotions by suppressing what is felt, what I'd rather focus on is what to do when the yucky feelings like sadness, frustration, anger, or fear emerge for your young professionals. (I suspect you and your young professional are just fine with the expression of the positive ones, so I'm going to leave those alone.)

According to Dr. Jill Bolte Taylor, a neuroanatomist who recreated cellular life on the left side of her brain after surviving a stroke at 37, we can move through our emotions most quickly if we play by the 90-second rule. People take 90 seconds to feel fully the emotion spawned from a negative event. Whether that "event" is someone yelling at us, a job loss, or even the death of a loved one, when the emotion swells within us we finish responding to the stress of it in just 90 seconds. Then our hormones—which produced the emotional reaction—return to their typical set point. If you continue to focus your thoughts on the situation that triggered the response, your body will go through the physiological process it did during those last 90 seconds all over again. And again and again if you keep your thoughts fixated on it. Redirect your thinking and you avoid a repeat of the emotional response.

Now here's the rub with much of the workplace thinking that says *not* to express your emotions. The more you think about not releasing the feeling, the more you think about the situation; and therefore, the more your body will go through an endless succession of 90-second cycles. For young professionals who take pride as a generation in their transparency—which includes being honest with their emotions—the quickest and most efficient way to help them process professionally what comes up for them is to encourage them to indulge in their 90 seconds. Let them take 90 seconds, either privately or with you, to sit and experience whatever they are feeling. Then, have them exhibit the control to redirect their thoughts back to opportunities, gifts, treasures, or whatever you want to call it and move on.

Hiring Manager Marcy Gives Young Professional Petros His 90 Seconds

Let's imagine that Marcy is like most hiring managers. She wants to see her staff succeed. She's onboarded a lot of young professionals over the last couple of years, and she's seen her fair share of tears and temper tantrums in the process. She's been through enough leadership training to have had it ingrained that successful, respected leaders don't lose their cool in the workplace. Yet Marcy is making her way through *90 Days 90 Ways* and is open to seeing if this 90 seconds thing really works. Explore how she applies it with one of her new hires, Petros, whom she observes is on the verge of an outburst during a conversation.

Marcy: Petros, I can't help but notice that you look like you're going to explode. What's going on?

Petros: I am so angry right now. I feel like if I say any more, something is going to come out of my mouth that will get me fired.

Marcy: I'm sorry you're feeling this way. You know this is a safe space. And I suspect that trying to suppress whatever is going on is just going to make you think about it longer and get in your own way of getting over it. What do you think?

Petros: Sounds fair enough.

Marcy: So with your permission, I'd like to discuss whatever it is for a minute or two just to get it out. How does that sound to you?

Petros: Great. But will it stay here? I don't want to come off as a tattletale or anything. Or piss people off more than they apparently already are.

Marcy: Mum's the word.

Petros: Okay, well, for the last two weeks as you know I've been working on the company magazine, which at first I was really happy about. I hoped coming here I'd have the chance to write some articles and do some editing and all of that has been happening really fast. But I've also wound up being a project manager, and I feel like I'm spending most of my time hounding people for their work so that we get the magazine out by the first of the month. I don't want to name names, but a lot of people couldn't care less about making the deadline and with it just 48 hours away for the mock-up I keep emailing them asking when I can expect their copy without hearing a word in return.

Marcy: What has your supervisor's role been in this?

Petros: So that's who I seriously had to control myself from going off on like five minutes ago. She had the nerve to tell me to stop pestering these certain people so that they could get their work done. And then, I can't even believe she said this, she told me that "some people" think that I'm too pushy. She told me, "I should just chill out a little bit." Yeah, it would be great to "chill out," but how the heck am I supposed to "chill out" when I know that if I don't have the mock-up by tomorrow I'm the one who will have failed to meet one of my major deadlines?! Must be easy to be so "chill," coming in to work late and scooting out a few hours early each day like she always does. It's so unfair, Marcy, and I'm totally at a loss about what I should do. I feel like I don't have any support from my team, and that they just couldn't care less about any of this. Though I guarantee when they all get yelled at from our director, they'll all be pointing fingers at me since I'm supposedly in charge yet I don't have any power in the situation.

> **Marcy:** How does it feel to get this all out? To vent?
>
> **Petros:** Surprisingly better.
>
> **Marcy:** Okay, while this might feel unnatural, I'm going to ask you to pause here. Let's put this away and come back together tomorrow to discuss once you've had some distance and can calm down. Now, let's completely change the subject so that you get back to being the you who sat in here less than a month ago over the moon about the opportunity to write. Tell me about the fabulous interview I heard you conducted with the VP of business development in our Macau office.

Marcy jumps in and stops Petros from getting himself stuck in the cycle of anger by going back into the same story. Like Marcy, you can keep your eye on the time and be responsible for directing young professionals' thinking away from their emotional trigger at the 90-second mark. Or, if you have worked with a new hire around the 90-second rule in the past, you can have them be responsible for stopping their 90-second emotional purge on their own. While your own comfort level with emotions will dictate whether you have young professionals sit with their emotions with you in conversation or on their own, what's important is engendering the habit to put thoughts back to possibilities after the big burst of emotion has had a chance to be released. Remember, drama queens (and kings) are made, not born!

DEVELOP PROACTIVITY OVER REACTIVITY

Oftentimes the kind of strong emotions that young professionals like Petros feel could have been avoided through a little smart work prior to their immersion in a project. Develop within your young professionals the ability to anticipate potential hiccups to success. Then, give them the ability to work proactively to minimize their impact.

Proactivity Vs. Reactivity

Proactivity and **reactivity** can both be defined as responding to mental, emotional, and behavioral stress. The difference is that when you are proactive you react *prior* to the actual encounter with the stressful trigger to mitigate against its negative impact on you down the line.

To make young professionals proactive, encourage them to ask three questions each time they take on a new project: *What are the likely problem points? What are the unlikely problem points? And what have I learned from past experiences to help me address the two?* Had Petros asked himself these questions at the start of his company magazine assignment, he would have identified that likely problems would be getting people to meet their deadlines—a problem for almost any person I've worked with in the world of marketing and communications—and a lack of respect for his authority. After all, he is the new kid on the block. Petros probably would have also realized that a less likely, yet still very possible problem would be his relationship with his supervisor. As he alluded to in his conversation with Marcy, Petros believes his supervisor is taking short cuts in her own work, coming in late and leaving early. Finally, let's imagine that Petros has a history with feeling a little broken when people critique him.

Having shined a light on the deadline, his relationship with his supervisor, and his fragile ego, Petros could have set himself—and his team—up better for success. First, he could have handled the deadlines with his other staff members differently. He could have set them earlier than needed to account for the possibility of extensions. And, while he might not have anticipated his supervisor telling him to "chill out," knowing that she is someone who can be—shall we say, a little lazy—he could have solicited her involvement on the front end. Whether she decided to take responsibility for the other writers making their deadlines or simply gave suggestions for how to help the team meet them, Petros would then have been able to go to her at any point and reference the agreement they had made together. Most importantly, had Petros been aware of his area for growth around his sensitivity, he could have received his supervisor's feedback with gratitude rather than resistance. And then, upon reflection, decide which pieces to keep and which to discard.

ZAP CONFLICT

DAY 60

Of course sometimes, even when best intentions meet a healthy dose of foresight, conflict happens. Most likely your young professionals hate conflict as much as you hated onboarding prior to page one! As we've discussed, they have typically had one of two firsthand encounters of it. If they grew up privileged, they had a lot of parental intervention so they never developed the skills to resolve conflict themselves. Or, if they were bullied in school or lived in a community where violence was a way of life, they probably have a warped reality of how conflict can be efficiently and effectively resolved. And if they have turned the TV on at all over the last few years, they've probably seen a whole lot of mismanagement of conflict from the people they should be looking to for examples. Whether it's from celebrities duking it out on their reality TV shows or Congress playing partisan politics, young professionals now need a healthy model of what effective conflict resolution looks like.

Let your young professionals know first and foremost that conflict is normal and that when it emerges, it's important to nip in the bud quickly before it erupts. Teach them that oftentimes conflict foments the more engaged people are with their work. For when we feel passionately, we have the desire to fight for our beliefs. Encourage young professionals to keep disagreements about ideas rather than people. To this end, as we discussed in the last chapter around negotiation, encourage them to ask questions rather than make assumptions. Oftentimes the darkest and dirtiest conflicts come from what is not asked rather than from what is.

When young professionals sense that something is foul, they will instinctually revert back to their early encounters with conflict by running to someone else to handle it or by pouncing on the other person. Curb whichever conflict mismanagement strategy is their go-to one quickly. Develop their ability to go from the symptom to the source—as we modeled in chapter 6—and most importantly, to focus on a mutually beneficial solution. As in a negotiation, it's important to know what each person needs to feel good about the outcome. Once this has been established, then young professionals can facilitate the resolution so that all implicated parties get their required takeaways.

When seeking to quell conflict, teach young professionals to give everyone time to cool off. Then, have them set a specific day, time, and place for the people in conflict to speak. Have them begin by giving everyone space to describe briefly how they feel. Then, before anyone gets caught up in her story, teach young professionals to move the conversation forward with questions such as "Where do we go from here? What's the outcome you're looking for?" Unlike a negotiation where a young professional can gain leverage from not showing all of her cards, in conflict the sooner they get to drafting a solution, the better. In order to go there, all parties need to know what others are hoping will happen next. Finally, have young professionals move the conversation from brainstorming to resolution by recapping the overlaps in solutions that have been proposed. Give everybody in the conversation an opportunity to articulate her role in implementing the outcome. And if you want your young professionals to be true class acts, drive home the importance of showing gratitude to the people who came to the table to devise a solution. Doing so helps repair potentially fractured relationships by restoring respect and helps everyone walk away more at peace.

BRING IN SOME OLD-FASHIONED FORGIVENESS

The most effective way to make conflict an aberration rather than a recurring theme for your young professionals is to get them moving forward once a solution has been reached. As we discussed earlier in the chapter, if young professionals can redirect their attention away from a negative emotional trigger after 90 seconds, it will end. But what happens when a young person is so attached to the story of how someone wronged her that she simply can't stop thinking about what that other person did? Or even worse, what if she—like many young professionals—has such high expectations for herself that she can't let get of the story of how *she* screwed up? For many young professionals, the biggest source of lingering conflict is their own self-narrative. Whether it's shifting how they have archived some negative feedback or were overlooked for an opportunity they felt they would be perfect for, a surefire way to get them from feeling crappy to feeling calm and recommitted to their work is for them to give everyone involved in a conflict a nice helping of forgiveness.

According to the Mayo Clinic, forgiveness is not just for the playground or for the faithful. It's as vital for sustainable physical health as it is for emotional and spiritual well-being. When you model and engender a culture of forgiveness, you are not playing Pollyanna or forgetting what has transpired. Rather, you are acknowledging each person's role, including your own, and then releasing everyone from the old problem. By doing so you redirect focus toward what is working—so that is what you actualize moving forward. You increase your empathy—which is a key facet of emotional intelligence and will prevent the development of future conflict. And perhaps most importantly, your individual act helps reduce the collective feeling of stress and tension throughout the workplace. It lowers your individual blood pressure and decreases your chances of depression, addiction, and chronic pain. And for young professionals who often create a narrative of conflict when they feel powerless, by making the choice to forgive they take back control over a situation. They move out of victimhood. They move into ethical leadership and see themselves the way they most want to be seen—as values-driven and virtuous.

KILL FEAR MONGERING

DAY 60

Okay, you may be thinking to yourself, "Enough about the fear already. I thought we were done with that." Not so fast. It's incomplete to talk about supporting young professionals in conflict, getting them focused on solutions, and helping them be forgiving without some discussion around fear as a form of bullying. As you saw with Petros in the earlier example, young professionals can be masterful fear mongers. From years of absorbing fear in western culture, it's easy for young professionals to derail themselves with if/then messages. "If _____ happens, then _____ will happen as a result." While we all can fall prey to this thinking, young professionals with limited work experience can create particularly high stakes for situations that just don't warrant them.

Young professionals are especially damaged when companies keep them living and working in a place of fear. While you may think it's benign or perhaps even a good thing for a young professional to believe that a missed deadline could be grounds for a termination, fear is a lousy motivator; yet it makes a really great performance killer. If a young professional directs focus toward speed at the expense of turning out a high-quality product, not only do you make underperformance acceptable and habitual, you quite likely set that young professional up to get a real lambasting! Similarly, if you allow young professionals to think about the negative—let's say the possibility of layoffs in a down economy—that person moving forward is going to be about half as present at work each day. The remaining 50 percent of her is going to be split between worrying about the possibility of unemployment, strategizing what to do if unemployment becomes a reality, and perpetuating the cycle of fear and crisis by planting worry in her peers. While you can and should be transparent about information when all facts are known, be aware of young professionals' inclination to magnify gloom and doom and spread it. Express potential dangers within the context of what can still go right. And, once you share them, move on.

When young professionals do sit with their fear, in addition to supporting them to have their 90 seconds in order to get back to a place of calm and positivity, encourage them to get real about the likelihood of their worst fears being realized. (The expression "False Expectations Appearing Real" is as accurate as it is humorous.) According to Dr. Susan Jeffers, author of the classic *Feel the Fear... And Do It Anyway,* "90 percent of what we worry about never happens. That means that our negative worries have less than a 10 percent chance of being correct." Encourage young professionals to realize that being positive is actually the more realistic response.

Of course, fear is not always rational. Admitting that it's unlikely doesn't always slay it. If they find they are repeating 90-second cycles of fear again and again like a catchy new song on their iPod, ask your young professionals to tease it out to its natural conclusion. In other words, if someone says they are scared about what will happen if they miss a deadline, ask her to keep asking herself, "Then, what would happen?" The answers, though ridiculous, usually show the person she could handle it. "If I miss the deadline, I'd get yelled at. I'd be embarrassed." Oftentimes it stops there, and the person realizes that a little egg on one's face is rotten but rarely ruinous. Even if the person goes into the terrain of, "I'd get fired. I'd go on unemployment. I'd have to move home with my parents. I'd have to start the job hunt all over again. I'd have to call all my friends and ask if there are any openings where they work," rarely is the end point "homelessness or death." And if it is, chances are that person needs some therapeutic intervention!

GET THEM ORGANIZED *THEIR* WAY

It's no secret that if you want to increase employee productivity you want employees to work in an environment that sets them up to do their best work. For young professionals who may be in their first or second workspace, it can take a bit of time to experiment before settling on what organization looks like for them. During the first couple of weeks as your new employees play around with their space, resist the temptation of turning into a parent and judging what to you might look like a mess, but is in fact a necessary part of their process to figure out how to make their space most functional. While you naturally want to encourage the minimization of clutter—for no matter who you are, looking at piles of papers and other mess fosters unnecessary tension—give young employees the time to find their order within what to you might look like a little madness. As young professionals are making decisions about how to design a work environment that makes them feel good and work smart, encourage them to think about the relationship between their computer, phone, files, document holders, calendar, vision board, and so forth, so that it is functional and calming.

Feng shui expert Elaine Wright has several recommendations for how you can honor many young professionals' desires to be taken seriously and work in a creative and calming space. With regard to the former, she suggests putting desks in a commanding position in a room with a view of the door. This enables people to feel in control of their work and know who is entering their space—qualities that young professionals appreciate. For young professionals engaged in any kind of creative work, Elaine suggests a desk with curves. She also notes that if you are seeking to foster a sense of balance, well-being, and inner alignment, a kidney-shaped desk can actually help create these feelings. She says plants, particularly green ones, can have a tremendous impact on creating a sense of calm within an office. They reduce the toxins present in a room, bring the outdoors in, and represent growth and development.

BE MINDFUL OF THE LEARNING CURVE

Just as young professionals need time to create a success inducing space, they also need time to get absorbed into your company culture and feel comfortable in their roles and accompanying tasks. According to Tyler Durbin, the founder of GenYJourney. com, when young professionals enter the workplace, the learning curve is not just about discovering how work gets done. It's also about understanding the resources that are available and trying to find one's individual place and ability to contribute within an organization. Whether young professionals are working at a start-up or a Fortune 500 company, they have a lot of processes to wrap their heads around. As Tyler explains, "Whether it's how to conduct meetings, collaborate on projects, or know where to find paper plates for lunch, processes are an integral part of how successful we are within the organization. It's perfectly fine to be a follower early in our careers. We learn by observing and listening to others. Once we have the necessities down, then we can step outside the box and up the ante with our contributions."

Honoring your young professional's learning curve is more about your own "being" as it is about any specific "doing." When you show up to each conversation, work assignment, or feedback session aware of what is likely going on for young professionals in their first quarter, you will naturally give them the support they need. Sometimes this will mean easing up on the workload. Other times it's bringing young professionals along to shadow at meetings. Or simply have an eye open toward potential signs of frustration and overwhelming feelings to address them early. The key is remembering that young professionals are not only reeling from being thrown into a new workplace. Oftentimes they are discovering their very first professional job. They are also learning what appropriate behavior and performance in the 21st century workplace looks like while reconciling their fears, hopes, and assumptions with their new reality.

ENCOURAGE OUTSIDE INTERESTS

As you read the title of this tactic, I suspect you did a double-take. Yes, if you want young professionals to be peak performers, then it's vital you give them permission to continue their robust leisure lives. I've had countless managers ask me, "Am I supposed to let my employees leave work whenever they feel like going to a yoga class or to coach a community basketball team?" Of course not, without a logical, mutually agreed upon plan for making up the missed time or work. Before making an assumption that a young professional employee is unwilling to fulfill her responsibilities and wants to be all play and no work, consider that she may simply be asking for support in sustaining her performance by getting her core need to have a life outside of work met.

Work-Life Balance Vs. Work-Life Integration

Work-life balance, like the name suggests, is equilibrium between work and the rest of one's life. As Rebecca Thorman, a prominent young professional career blogger explains, the relationship between work and life is more like a "seesaw, kind of up and down, and is only ever balanced for the briefest moments in time." **Work-life integration** is the process of honoring the needs of employees and their families by removing the dichotomy between career and personal life and creating opportunities, programs, and services for richness and overlap in these areas.

Like their more senior employees, most young professionals recognize that it is unrealistic to achieve balance between the various facets of one's life. Therefore, integration is the goal. Rather than scolding your new hires for seeking to be engaged outside of the workplace, laud them for it. Engagement is infectious. When you help people cultivate it in one aspect of their life, typically it spreads to the other areas.

VALUE PRIVACY AND "OFF" TIME

DAY 45

In order for young professionals to enjoy work-life integration, they need to have opportunities to detach from email, social media, and work. Establish with young professionals healthy boundaries between work and the other areas of their life, so that they and you are clear. For example, can you mutually agree that emails will not be sent over the weekend? Or, if they are, that they are to be read and not responded to?

It's equally important to show young professionals how to be "off" within the course of the workday. There will likely be times when they need permission to shut their doors or not pick up their phones so that they can focus on higher-level creative work. Establish the appropriate means for doing this. For example, a lot of managers complain that their young professionals have iPod buds on their ears at their desks. While this may be inappropriate for your workplace, particularly if it's a staple of how that young professional works as a way to block out excessive noise when it arises, unpick why it—or some similar distancing habit—is happening prior to drawing conclusions. It's quite possible that young professional is signaling she needs a way to focus. If this is the case, strategize a more mutually agreeable way, for example, putting a friendly sign in front of one's cubicle, "Please respect that I'm taking some quiet time. I look forward to chatting with you later," or establishing certain hours each day where someone is not expected to be checking email, and so forth.

The workplace does not serve anyone when it is a stress-inducing environment, or when it prevents employees from enjoying their hours off the clock. Stress + hard work *does not* create a productive employee. On the contrary, stress costs American companies approximately $300 billion each year in absenteeism, presenteeism (coming to work despite illness), lackluster performance, poor company morale, and turnover. While CEOs and senior leaders often see their anxiety as testaments to their work ethics, stressful feelings are often less a sign of achievement or a feature of one's professional role than a measurement of one's not so useful response to it. For employees to create company calm, they need daily opportunities for happiness, leisure, learning, growth, and a sense of accomplishment. New hires who become peak performers must be able to nourish themselves with positive people, beliefs, and thoughts; have time each day to dedicate to their self-care; and have created or ascended to roles where they feel like they do good work and can continue to evolve.

Tweet-Sized Takeaways

- Model possibility-centered thinking and support young professionals to find the opportunity within every obstacle.
- Give young professionals 90 seconds to experience their feelings and then redirect their focus away from the emotional trigger.

- Foster young professionals' proactivity by giving them three questions to ask at the start of any project.

- Teach young professionals that conflict is normal and give them the tools to resolve it quickly and effectively when it erupts.

- Get young professionals to see forgiveness as an act of ethical leadership.

- Remind young professionals that while fear is normal, choosing to see the positive is usually the more realistic choice.

- Support young professionals to design a workspace that empowers them, supports creativity, and encourages calmness.

- Keep your young professional's learning curve in mind at all times.

- Honor your young professional's desire for work-life integration.

- Co-create strategies and techniques for young professionals to be "off" so they can focus on higher level work.

chapter 10

Inspire Great Performance

"Our mission statement about treating people with respect and dignity is not just words but a creed we live by every day. You can't expect your employees to exceed the expectations of your customers if you don't exceed the employees' expectations of management."

Howard Schultz

You've probably realized by now that this book is as much about *your* development as it is about what to *do* to make your young professionals successful. As I've shared with you previously, one of my favorite coaching questions when anyone I speak with complains about the "other" person—whether the other is a supervisor, colleague, client, romantic partner, family member, and so forth—is "What's your role in that?" And in your pursuit of onboarding young professionals efficiently and effectively to be successful within the realities of the 21st century workplace, your role in their development is *huge*. Given that most of the competencies you are seeking to build incorporate mindset and behavior as much if not more so than particular tasks you are seeking for them to execute, it's important that you are living, breathing, and being all of the qualities you are seeking to engender so that you create a culture where they can grow and thrive. In addition to employing the strategies and corresponding tactics in the preceding chapters, if you want to grow a new generation of peak performers, you need to demonstrate daily what such performance looks like.

BE A MIRROR FOR WHAT YOU SEEK

I imagine you are probably thinking, "being a mirror for peak performance sounds good, but how do I actually do this in practice?" Before we go deeper into the art of inspiring performance from your young professionals, I'm going to ask you to take a moment and answer a question. "How can I be the [insert your role] that I wanted when I was launching my career?" Whether your hiring manager, supervisor, trainer, or coach was exactly what you hoped for, the furthest thing from it, or more likely somewhere in between, get clear on what could have best enabled your success—as well as what enables your success currently. For when you know what you yearn for, you will be much more likely to give other people what they need.

I once spoke at an HR conference where somebody in the audience brought up her young professionals' unrealistic expectations. (And in case you're not already two steps ahead of me, I'm pretty clear she had not thought a lot about what supports *her* success.) When I asked the woman to share with me what she meant, she explained, "They just think that everything is supposed to be fun and games. And that's just not the way work gets done. This isn't preschool." A couple of things came up for me when I heard this response. First, I was really glad I wasn't working for the woman. She had an advanced case of obstacle-centered thinking. Second, before I risked putting my foot in my mouth, I needed the woman to explain her own expectations for her young professionals. She answered, "That they show up eager to play their role. That they go above and beyond what I ask them to do, like I used to do for my supervisor. I would put in 60–70 hour work weeks when I first started here, and I haven't stopped."

Before I could say anything, chuckles erupted in the audience. The woman had confirmed my suspicion and mostly likely theirs. Her expectations were just as unrealistic as the expectations she believed her young professionals were holding. So I asked the woman, from a place of love rather than judgment, "What has been the payoff for working so hard?" She stood somewhat dumbstruck, and then confessed, "You know, I have absolutely no idea. Having a job, I guess."

My heart broke for this woman. She wanted so desperately for her young professionals to subscribe to her set of beliefs, and yet she had no idea if or how her beliefs had served her. Sure, she had a steady paycheck, several weeks paid vacation each year, and would most likely enjoy a decent retirement package for her lifetime of service. However, there was no indication she enjoyed the work she did. Or that she believed she was making any difference in the world. Or most importantly, that she enjoyed the life her job had given her. Projecting all of this onto her young professionals, she was most likely the number one reason her young staff were underperforming. The last thing they wanted was to wind up like her.

As a key player in the onboarding of young professionals, your every thought, belief, relationship, action, and achievement is going to be dissected. When you mirror who and what calls to young professionals—whether that's by being someone who has made a positive social impact or is perceived to be an ethical leader—your young professionals will follow you wherever you take them. On the flip side—if you show up to work focused on the obstacles, talk poorly of your colleagues, or fail to listen to the people around you—they will do exactly the opposite of what you want from them. Wouldn't you? What person follows a model that she sees leading toward professional and personal dissatisfaction?

LET YOURSELF LEARN FROM THEM

If I had the opportunity to speak again with the woman mentioned in the previous tactic, I would ask her, "What have you learned from your young professionals?" For good onboarding, just like good leadership, revolves around spiral learning—as much for the people leading the process as for the people "following" it.

> **Aa** **Spiral learning** is the art and practice of revisiting concepts to deepen insight and skill building through each additional exposure to content.

For your young professionals this means they need multiple opportunities to encounter your deployment of the strategies and corresponding tactics in the book. For *you*, it means that to make top-notch onboarding second nature, you need to keep doing it to improve your own performance. You also want to be open to what your young professionals can teach you to strengthen your work.

One of the things that most entertains me in intergenerational workplace conversations is when a member of a generation—young or old—gripes about a different generation. And then, in the same breath, that person expresses that one of her areas for growth is a strength that that "other" generation is typically strong in. Think for a moment about one of your areas for growth. If you've been developing new employees for any period of time, I'm going to go out on a limb and posit that you may be struggling to maintain work-life integration. You may be somewhat resistant to change. And most likely your personal brand and your strategy for sharing it could use some tweaking. You see where I'm going, yes? Your young professionals may have the insight to help you in the areas *you* need.

When you allow yourself to learn and grow from your young professionals, a bunch of beautiful things happen. First, the obvious, you give yourself the gift of self-development. You get re-energized in your work and perform better in your role. Also, you send some powerful messages to your young professionals. You demonstrate that you are as committed to your development as you expect your new hires to be committed to theirs. This is a potent form of sustaining your young professional's initial inspiration. It makes humility cool. It honors the young professional value to make an impact and develop their leadership—the latter which we'll come back to in the second to last tactic. It gives young professionals an opportunity to see themselves as masters of particular content. Perhaps most importantly, it highlights the areas of commonality between employees of different generations rather than repeatedly reinforcing differences. Remember, learning from your youngest employees also includes little things: discovering a new application for your smartphone, recognizing an opportunity to serve in your community, or understanding the importance of working in a team rather than going at a new project alone. The key is seeing your young professionals—and treating them—as people capable of making a variety of important contributions.

MAKE YOURSELF ACCESSIBLE

Make it easy for your young professionals to grab time with you beginning day one—if not before. (Nothing warms new hires' hearts more than when a member of the onboarding team, ideally a direct supervisor, reaches out prior to the official start date.) It affirms that they have made the right choice in coming to work for you because they will be a part of a community that genuinely cares about who they are—important stuff, remember, for young professionals who are drawing big conclusions about their tenure with you in their first days. Moving forward, continue to reach out informally to show your continued interest and support. Schedule weekly time to check in. Let your young professionals have access to your calendar be it physically placed somewhere accessible—if you're old school like me and still like paper—or online. Encourage them to book dedicated time with you as needed irrespective of the reason.

Hand-Holding vs. Face Time

Hand-holding is when you actually *do* the mental, physical, or spiritual work for another person or provide so much oversight that you might as well just be doing it yourself. When you let yourself be present early and often to young professionals, giving them what I like to refer to as "**face time**," the last thing you do is take over the reins. Instead, you lend a supportive ear. Sometimes young professionals simply need to talk out loud. Other times, they will want to dump frustrations. And on rarer occasions than they're given credit for, they will want to cry "uncle" and receive some coaching. You are supporting them to be in full control of their performance and the achievement of results, starting with sharing their load with you—their way—so that they don't ever get buried underneath it.

I don't want to assume that when you began reading this tactic you were thinking that I was suggesting you hold your young professionals' hands. But if you were, read the above distinction again and really get it into your bones. The reason you make yourself accessible to young professionals is so that they can determine if/how you can set them up to succeed—now, and as a result, in the future. You make it easy for them to be proactive in their problem solving by deciding when, how, and regarding what they come to you for. Most importantly, by just being available, you are showing your young staff that you always have their backs.

GIVE THE GIFT OF TRUST

DAY 1

A 2010 study from Badenoch and Clark, a recruiting company in the United Kingdom, showed that approximately 32 percent of Millennials don't trust senior management at their organizations. While the study may have been conducted in the United Kingdom, I suspect it could have just as easily been undertaken in the United States and revealed similar results. For your young professionals, trust is really a quid pro quo. By making yourself present—rather than absent or overbearing—you certainly help young professionals feel trusted, which in turn helps them to trust you. In addition, in pursuit of getting your young professionals to trust you and your company, continue to show them how their work is integral to the achievement and sustenance of workplace vision, mission, and values. Be a person of your word—speaking up and out for what you believe in. Make choices that are consistent with the beliefs you purport to possess. And tell the truth—even when it's not pretty. Your young professionals will see your transparency as a testament to your trust in them and trust *you* more for it.

Creating a culture of mutual trust is vital to the young professional onboarding experience. Not only is it the backbone of retention, but it is also a key catalyst to their performance. Recruiting specialist, Scott Degraffenreid, suggests it might be the most effective form of workplace recognition—above a fancy title or pay increase. I agree. I'll never forget when a former director told me she was going to be out of town for the culmination of a big yearly project our department ran and was leaving me to step into her role. While this experience could have just as easily been an anecdote I dropped into a tactic about pushing your young professional outside her comfort zone, letting her go, or preparing her for leadership, I'm intentionally putting it into trust. For when my director showed through her actions that she trusted me completely with her "baby," that was the moment I decided I would lay myself down on railroad tracks for her, and really my entire company, if asked. Up until that point I'd been having a lot of doubts about my potential for upward mobility, my opportunity to make the maximum possible impact—yada yada yada—yet in that single act, all of that fear melted away. While there were no guarantees what the future at the company would hold for me, I finally trusted in the adage that "hard work pays off."

 ## PUSH YOUNG PROFESSIONALS OUTSIDE THEIR COMFORT ZONES

It's widely accepted business philosophy that employees do their best work when pushed outside of their comfort zones—as long as they are given the support to be able to thrive in it. Former GE CEO Jack Welch is perhaps the most outspoken proponent of such practice, for years notoriously laying off seasoned middle managers who refused to step into the unknown and stretch into their greatness. In fact, current GE CEO Jeff Immelt credits his current job title to such a push from when he was just 33 years old. Welch and the HR chief at the time, Bill Conaty, saw Immelt's leadership potential and brought him in to manage the recall of one million faulty refrigerators, which was a daunting project for even the most seasoned executive leader. Clearly, Immelt passed the test!

Young professionals used to have a lot of these "stretch assignments" in their initial days with a company. This could mean having six months to a year of rotational roles within the corporate office of their organization—which allowed them to understand the inner workings of each facet of the company and opened up the possibility for future upward and lateral growth within it—or the chance to compete for a short-term global placement. In either format, these opportunities let young professionals step into and experience the unknown. As a result, young professionals learned how to tap into themselves to devise sound solutions to problems they had likely never encountered before. They had the opportunity to build deep relationships with the people they were immersed with. They exponentially grew their leadership abilities. And of course, they positioned themselves for progressively responsible positions within their companies.

Unfortunately, many of these roles were the first to be cut during the most recent economic downturn. As a general rule, young professionals are being kept for longer periods of time in entry-level roles where they are focused on short-term tasks. This not only has a negative impact on their career trajectory, it also stymies an organization's leadership pipeline. You can—and should—give young professionals opportunities to stretch within any role they hold even if your company has done away with more formal developmental assignments. Ideally, you design a stretch assignment around the career development goals you have established with your young professional so that she can develop specific, measurable, and relevant skills and behaviors. Here are a few examples of stretch assignments for young professionals that I encourage you both to steal and let jump-start your own ideas.

- Create a company culture video for future new hires.

- Participate in a two- to four-week lateral job swap with a young professional in a different department.

- Propose a solution for increasing revenue or decreasing expenses by a particular amount or percentage for a project/program.

- Represent the company at a trade show or conference.

- Design and manage a company social media page/profile.

- Plan a recruitment event for a local college, university, or trade school.

- Organize a team community service day.

LET EMPLOYEES HAVE INPUT

DAY 60

Another important area for most young professionals to continue to stretch, as we spent a chapter discussing, is their interpersonal communication. Give new employees the opportunity to have input—in everything from the setup of their workspace and hours they'll work, to the projects they will take on and their roles in them. By doing so you give them the opportunity to rehearse and refine their practice of sharing a persuasive case. Just as importantly, you make them feel valuable and increase their sense of commitment to their work. Remember, they are used to having parents seek their opinions and advice on everything from family vacations to major purchases like computers and cars.

When young professional Cher Hale was hired on as a director for the social enterprise Hero School, she says she had the luxury of giving input in everything from her job description, to her chief responsibilities, to new projects Hero School would pursue. Cher says that this freedom "increased my engagement and performance tenfold. Since I'm working on the things that interest me, I'm always excited about my projects." Cher's input has also had a significant positive impact on Hero School and its community. "When I was first hired, I realized that there weren't any processes in place for onboarding volunteers, so I was able to create a volunteer package that helped them understand our mission and future goals." This of course made it easier for volunteers to do their work with Hero School and spread the word for and about the group.

The key to asking for input, irrespective of when you solicit it, is making sure you genuinely want to hear it. The only thing worse for a young professional than not having the space to share her opinion is being told to give it, and then, upon sharing it, having it devalued. I'll never forget back in my theatre days when I watched a director tell a young actor, "I'm going to take your idea and put it in my pocket." The condescension still speeds up my heart rate almost a decade later! Let your young professionals know exactly what you are going to do with their two cents—sans any reference to putting it in your pocket and implying it will intentionally get lost in your spin cycle. Perhaps you will be bringing it to a team meeting for further discussion. Run some numbers over the next couple of weeks to test its feasibility. Whatever choice you make, be transparent about it. This will enable your young professionals to know when and how to look for the impact of their idea.

PROSELYTIZE MENTORSHIP

DAY 90

While working with a mentor is an important career and performance enhancement strategy for a professional of any age or level of experience, it is particularly beneficial for someone near the start of her career. Most likely your young professionals want more feedback and learning and growth opportunities than an individual supervisor, manager, or trainer can give them. Mentoring relationships can alleviate some of the pressure from those most responsible for a young professional's performance. It facilitates the opportunity to have honest conversations with people not so directly attached to the outcome. Mentoring relationships also provide prescriptive recommendations for career and workplace success based on tested strategies and lived experience.

To best support young professionals in finding a mentor (or mentors)—which can often be easier said than done—help them identify what they most want, for example: someone who has taken a nontraditional path to leadership, maintained work-life integration from the C-Suite, or who gives laser-like feedback. It may be that you can facilitate the connection for the person internally or from your personal network. And if nothing else, simply by helping young professionals identify the significance of finding mentors and clarifying their mentoring priorities, they will likely start to identify possible people to whom they can reach out.

For Ryan McMahan, his relationships with his mentor evolved over time—like it does for a lot of young professionals. "My boss happened to live down the street from me so we started running together in the mornings," he explains. "When she and I became friends, I had just been out of college for a year and navigating the workplace was still pretty new to me. She did a lot in terms of helping me find my strengths and figure out exactly what kind of work I want to be doing." Ryan explains that his mentor also helped him develop his professional skills and behaviors. "I tend to have a personality where if someone doesn't understand me, I'm not always so understanding about that. She helped me learn how to better communicate *with* people, manage *my* expectations, and overall just develop my soft skills." Perhaps most importantly for Ryan, his mentor has become both a friend and an advocate. "I go to her before making any big decision, and even though we don't work together anymore, we still do calls about once a month."

In his current role as Operational Manager—interestingly enough at iMentor, an organization that prepares high school students from underserved communities for college success through technology-enabled mentoring—Ryan continues to see the benefits of his mentoring relationship. "When I was at City Year, there was a period where we were going through a lot of change, and I got to see how my mentor handled all of that. Now at iMentor, my job is all about keeping people happy and managing relationships. Internal customer service, where I am, is all about change. I learned a ton from my mentor about how to work with people, no matter the situation."

Katharine Bierce, a young professional at Opera Solutions, found one of her mentors, a principal in her company, even more organically—from chatting at the copy machine. Katharine recommends that anyone new on the job use the line, "Have I met you before?" whenever she sees someone she doesn't know. In Katharine's case, "A two-minute 'hello' by the photocopier turned into a solid two hours of discussions and advice on how to move my project forward. This mentor provided a level of strategy that informed the first draft of a process model I designed. I also feel more confident in my work because I know I can bounce ideas off of a supportive and constructively critical principal before I have to present to other senior leaders."

For Katharine, some of her greatest learning and growth has come from her interactions with her mentors. After finishing a project early, one mentor took Katharine out "for what became a three-hour dinner, where he shared a lot of useful advice about how to keep various people happy (and what makes some people annoyed, and how to avoid that)." Katharine says that when you have a great mentor who is a respected leader, it lets you see yourself for more than just your "number-crunching skills to the firm." Another one of Katharine's mentors has given her "some real gems of advice about how to run different kinds of meetings, depending on what the goal of the meeting is and who the stakeholders are. I'll be using that advice for the rest of my life," Katharine says.

Katharine believes having a mentor who is established within your company is also a great way to gain face time with senior level personnel. "One thing that takes some getting used to" for new grads, she explains, "is that you're *not* supposed to talk to some people directly. When you have a senior level person advocate for you rather than talk to the target decision maker directly, you avoid having that target decision maker write you off as being 'too junior' and therefore not valuable."

INVEST IN THEIR LEARNING AND DEVELOPMENT

DAY 90

Here's the good news. According to a 2011 SHRM poll, 44 percent of respondents said that they have implemented or increased their coaching for non-managers. And approximately 40 percent have upped their job training for new hires. Now, I don't want you to label me a killjoy, but it would be irresponsible for me not to also mention the flip side to all of this. As a result of the recession, the 2010 ASTD *State of the Industry* reported that those organizations surveyed experienced an approximately 6.1 percent drop in learning and development spending from the year before. And employees in the surveyed organizations participated in an average of just 31.9 hours of formal learning content over the course of a year, down from 36.3 hours in 2008. Not a tremendous decline, but a decline nonetheless. While I suspect that investments in learning and development will rebound in the next couple of years, the real lasting change is happening in the delivery of learning and development programs. Almost 37 percent of workplace learning is now happening via technology, and approximately 28 percent of it specifically through e-learning courses.

When Sodexo redesigned their award-winning onboarding program, they realized how many more touches they could have with their new staff if they put more of their training online. In "Come Alive with Sodexo," their one-year program for new managers, Sodexo puts company overview and compliance information into online, self-study modules for staff to complete within their first three months, for example: food and physical safety, ethics, information security, and customer standards. Then, employees can come together toward the end of the first quarter for face-to-face sessions that allow for more meaningful employee relationship building as well as targeted breakout sessions in various facets of leadership development. After this live event, employees return to online learning for core courses in business skill and staff development. Then, once they have encountered the general information, Sodexo employees again meet face-to-face for more specialized work in such areas as emotional intelligence, giving recognition, and career and self-development.

Young professionals *love* learning and development, and a keen L&D program is an easy and effective way to recruit and retain them. And if you can include life coaching as a component, all the better—at least according to Zappos employees. Zappos sees having an on-staff life coach as the key both to happy and successful employees. As Dr. Vik, Zappos' original life coach puts it, "How can an upset worker be productive?" Recognizing that there is no separation for people between their work and life, Zappos' life coaching gives employees an opportunity to address problems in any of the life spheres and develop the thoughts and feelings that are integral to workplace success. All employees are encouraged to take advantage of life coaching to set their goals and strategize how to achieve them. And by the sounds of it, most do. According to Zappos employee Melissa L., "I speak for quite a few when I say that [without our resident life coach] we wouldn't have the confidence or support to be the people that we are today."

Whether your organization is small and lacks the resources to formally invest in professional and personal development programming, or you have an onsite life coach like Zappos and fully realized virtual and face-to-face talent development programs for your staff like Sodexo, some of the best investments you can make in your young professionals will happen outside of your four walls. When young professionals have opportunities to develop with other young people they don't come into contact with daily, they have the space and safety to take bigger risks. They are exposed to new people and ideas. And oftentimes they can make discoveries about *who* they are and who they are in the process of becoming, which just aren't possible with people who already have assumptions and expectations about them based on their previous work history. While your community undoubtedly has development programs and networking groups specifically geared toward young professionals—and if you're stuck, check out your Chamber of Commerce, many have their own young professionals groups for emerging leaders—here are a sampling of external learning and growth opportunities I've been involved with to consider for your young professionals:

StartingBloc Institute for Social Innovation—http://www.StartingBloc.org

Each year in three to four cities across the world, StartingBloc brings together cohorts of approximately 100 emerging leaders and gives them access to the resources and training needed to harness business solutions to create lasting positive social impact. The transformative experience includes a survey of social innovation, an innovative case-study competition, and sessions with industry leaders.

Coach U—http://www.CoachU.com

I'm not telling you to send all of your young professionals to get certified as a coach. But if you want employees who make a habit of shifting obstacles into opportunities, know how to ask great questions, listen keenly, and are solution-oriented, I am suggesting that you expose them to the world of coaching. Coach U's four-week virtual class, "Becoming a Coach," is a low-cost, effective option.

The Woodhull Institute for Ethical Leadership—http://www.Woodhull.org

The Woodhull Institute's signature weekend retreats in upstate New York and San Francisco are designed for women in their 20s and 30s looking to develop the skills to be successful in business, politics, the community, and family life. Participants receive hands-on training in ethics and leadership development, public speaking, negotiation, voice, and financial literacy.

Brazen Careerist—http://www.BrazenCareerist.com

Brazen Careerist is the network for ambitious young professionals to connect and grow. They offer a range of free and low-cost virtual learning programs for young professionals as well as online speed networking, which they call Network Roulette. In addition to their programming for young professionals, Brazen facilitates virtual recruiting events that connect young professionals with recruiters in real-time, online conversations.

Step Into Your Moxie—http://www.StepIntoYourMoxie.com

In addition to my programs for organizations, I also lead virtual and face-to-face programs for women to develop the mindset, behaviors, and skills to better listen to their inner voices, sculpt their powerful messages, and speak them with confidence and competence in all areas of their lives. Taking the form of one-on-one coaching, tele-classes, live events, and a yearlong MasterTreat™ (think mastermind meets retreat), if you have young women ready to develop into high-impact, heart-centered communicators, send them my way!

PROVIDE OPPORTUNITIES TO LEAD

DAY 90

One of my leadership role models is Punam Mathur, the VP of employee and community engagement at NV Energy. The reason that I both respect and look to Punam as a paragon of "good" leadership is because she understands that what she possesses in title, everyone needs to feel within her role. "100 percent of people need to view themselves as leaders," she says. "Budgets in employee investment have been slashed. Often that's just the way it is. So we've got to get creative about how we build people up and develop the behaviors they need to reach our outcomes."

Punam believes that her responsibility is to give her staff opportunities to step into leadership so that they feel like they are making a contribution, and, of course, so that they actually can make one. I could easily write an entire chapter just on the tactics Punam uses firsthand and teaches her managers. One of my favorite ways that she has developed NV Energy leaders is by starting Toastmaster chapters within the company. The lunchtime meetings, to quote Punam, have been "wildly successful and hugely impactful," particularly for her young professionals who are looking to develop and position themselves for leadership.

Active on a number of community boards, Punam also encourages her young employees to spearhead service projects. The company was recently committed to an event for veterans, and Punam needed someone to take over the reins. The young person who did organized such an outstanding event that when a new management position opened up in client services shortly after, this young woman proved herself a natural fit for it. This employee, Punam is sure to make clear, "was not someone who had previously demonstrated leadership skills. We would have never pegged her as someone to have our eye on. The key is to keep giving pathways to people so they can surprise us. And for Millennials, that means hitting that 'refresh' button and making the old seem new again."

Katharine Bierce also believes some of her greatest leadership development has been through her opportunities to spearhead service projects at work. In her first quarter, Katharine learned that her company's Women in Business group facilitated volunteering and guest speaker events. She organized an internal volunteering day with New York Cares as well as the group's guest speaker for the same month. Afterward, she started a monthly global conference call for fellow employees interested in giving back to the community. Katharine boasts, "We currently have events every one to three months in the New York/New Jersey area!" From her philanthropic activities, Katharine has developed the ability to connect people to one another and to their local communities. She has also found a way to work intrapreneurially, feeding her entrepreneurial spirit. Katharine loves that she can create whatever she wants "as long as it doesn't impact [her] ability to deliver on assigned client/project work."

 _____

Remember in the introduction when I told you that this was *your* book? When I explained that while I was your guide in filling your toolbox with strategies and techniques for top-notch onboarding, ultimately it was *your* opportunity and responsibility to adopt the material to make it best work for you? Therefore, it's only appropriate that *you* name the final tactic for inspiring great performance in your young professionals.

Think about your values, your strengths, your resources, and your enthusiasms. What do you either currently do that you want to reinforce, or do you know you are ready to commit to start doing to develop the next generation of employees in your company? Perhaps you want to revisit the preceding chapters to identify a tenth tactic for one of the strategies. Or maybe there's an area I didn't touch upon that for your company is important to shine a light on. Whatever thought or feeling is coming up for you, follow it to its conclusion. You've stuck with me up until now, after all! And once you create and name the tactic, please share it—with the rest of your onboarding team, colleagues, and on social media (and if you're on Twitter—the hashtag for the book is #90d90w). Best practices get even better when they are shared!

Tweet-Sized Takeaways

- **Your young professionals are a direct reflection of you. If you don't like what you see, identify your role in what you're seeing.**

- **When you learn from your employees, you empower you and them.**

- **Make yourself accessible to employees so that they can reach out when they need you. This makes you a partner versus a parent.**

- **Trust is a quid pro quo for young professionals. If you want it from them, give it to them.**

- **Push young professionals outside their comfort zone to help them stretch into their next level of performance success.**

- **When young staff share their ideas, they enhance their communication skills, feel more responsibility for their work, and take pride in what they create.**

- **Match young professionals with mentors so they can learn prescriptive recommendations for career and workplace success.**

- **Invest in formal and informal learning programs within and outside your four walls.**

- **The future of your business, your country, and your world lies in the hands of your young professionals. Set them up to lead. Now!**

- **Take responsibility for transferring your learning into action by devising your own tactic for inspiring great performance.**

Afterthought

"What you have to give, you offer least of all through what you say; in greater part through what you do; but in greatest part through who you are."

Bob Burg and John David Mann

There is no "right" way to grow extraordinary young professionals. I have done my best to share the nine strategies and 90 corresponding tactics (including yours!) that I have seen work. To recap, they include:

- Create a knockout day one.

- Give them what they need to know to succeed.

- Integrate them into your workplace culture.

- Build high-impact communicators.

- Ensure a return on your expectations.

- Keep their focus on their focus.

- Develop impeccable customer service skills.

- Grow employees who create company calm.

- Inspire great performance.

What's most important, though, is that you figure out what works best for *your* people. And then you do it—early and often.

In their book, *It's Not About You: A Little Story About What Matters Most in Business*, authors Bob Burg and John David Mann not only pen one of my favorite pieces of advice, which I shared with you above; they also give one of the most succinct and spot-on summaries of the responsibility of a leader—you.

"As a leader, you become the container of others' hopes. When we say people put their trust in *you*, that is exactly what happens. They place their hopes and dreams, trust and faith, even their fears, in your hands, because these things feel too fragile, too big, too important, too valuable to hold onto by themselves...But, you are *not* their dreams, you are only the *steward* of those dreams. And leaders too often get it backwards and start thinking they not only *hold* the best of others but that they are that best."

As I have said throughout the book, your young professionals are the generation that will dominate the workplace by 2016. And while I really am an opportunity-centered person, I'm also realistic. My generation will likely be pressed to solve larger scale social, economic, and environmental problems than any previous generation. And they will have to do it at a younger age. At least in the United States, as citizens make clear they want a reduced role for federal and state government, our businesses will need to be the innovators and problem solvers. Your young professionals will soon be the ones charged with solving our energy crisis. Protecting communities from natural disasters. Responding to a financially unsustainable healthcare system. Creating jobs for a global workforce.

Your responsibility moving forward—as someone who takes young professionals from new hire to peak performer—is twofold. From the moment your young professionals say "yes" to their job offer, you are equally the "steward for their dreams" as well as the developer of their future stewardship. Your professional legacy is what they leave behind. Identify what behaviors and skill sets your company's leaders will need to make our current economic crises footnotes in history rather than recurring themes. Then, start developing those competencies within your young professionals in their first quarter. You know how much it will mean to them. Now, I trust you also see what it will mean to you, your company, and let's face it—our world.

Acknowledgments

I am a lucky gal to be able to show up to my life each day and engage in work that lets me leave the legacy I want to make. Thank you to the companies, colleges, conferences, and individual clients who have invited me in, embraced my message, and invested their trust in me. To those of you who have shared your best practices, stories, and challenges, this book is because of you.

Thank you to my brilliant writer friends, particularly Jon, Jacquette, Jess, and Emily. You have helped me navigate this process with equal parts creativity and calm. Your suggestions, questions, and most of all your ability simply to hold space and allow me to find my own answers has been such a gift.

I am lucky to have made the most innovative and resilient community in the country my home base. Las Vegas, thank you for taking me back and giving me so many opportunities. Thank you, particularly, for opening coffee shops and communal workspaces across the valley just in time for me to write this book, and for making the commitment to embed start-ups, sustainability, social change, and spirituality into our community DNA.

To my mentors: Jille, Punam, Mitalene, and Chris, whether we speak bimonthly or biyearly, your voice is always in my head…in the very best way.

My sincerest gratitude goes out to my team at ASTD Press—particularly Justin, Kristin, Heidi, and Ron. Thank you for shepherding this project from vision to actualization. You've made me very proud to be a card-carrying member of this organization.

Rita, thank you for embracing me from the moment you received the first draft of my book proposal. I appreciate your ability to bring out my best voice, champion my work, and always represent my interests.

Finally, who I am begins and ends with my family. Thank you, ALL of you, for your fierce cheerleading and boundless love. Much aloha to you, Stephen, for giving me the opportunity each day to be a better partner than I ever imagined I could be.

About the Author

Since winning the Miss Junior America competition as a college freshman, Alexia has been engaged in developing next generation talent. An in-demand speaker, International Coach Federation (ICF) certified coach, trainer, and media personality, Alexia specializes in helping organizations recruit, retain, educate, and grow their young professional workforce. Alexia's unique approach to talent development which fuses coaching, interactive role play, and her infectious sense of humor has made her an asset to a range of industries. From education to health care to nonprofits to the corporate sector, Alexia is shifting the way companies, professional associations, and colleges across the country develop their people.

Alexia is the author of *Awaken Your CAREERpreneur: A Holistic Road Map to Climb from Your Calling to Your Career* and has been featured by over 100 media outlets including CNN, NBC, *Wall Street Journal*, CBS MoneyWatch, FOX Business News, Forbes.com, ABCNews.com, TheGlassDoor.com, and Mint.com. Alexia is a proud member of the Young Entrepreneurs Council (YEC), an invite-only organization of the world's top entrepreneurs. Alexia recently launched a new brand, Step Into Your Moxie, through which she provides one-on-one and group coaching, weekend intensives, and a yearlong MasterTreat™ for professional women who want to develop their interpersonal communication, negotiation, presentation, and influencing skills.

Alexia is a leader in both her local ASTD and ICF chapters. She serves on the Advisory Council for the Vegas Young Professionals of the Las Vegas Chamber of Commerce and on the board of Family and Child Treatment (FACT) of Southern Nevada. A poster child for the values of Generation Y, Alexia lives with her husband Steve in a solar house, drives a Prius, meditates daily, practices yoga, and drinks a lot of green juice.

To bring Alexia to your organization, book her as a speaker, or get on her list to receive weekly tips for effective communication and leadership development, visit www. AlexiaVernon.com. You can also follow Alexia on Twitter @AlexiaVernon.

Index